Tonight, We Wrestle

Healing What You've Been Hiding

Donald A. Wright, Ph.D.

Foreword by T.D. Jakes

A revelation of theological treatment for the shattering
crisis of adult males hopelessly trapped
in boyhood to the dilemma of women in search of
"sensitive" ministry from their husbands.

Treasure House

a division of

Destiny Image

P.O. Box 310

Shippensburg, PA 17257

ISBN 1-56043-816-9

For Worldwide Distribution
Printed in the U.S.A.

Treasure House books are available through these fine distributors outside the United States:

Christian Growth, Inc.,
Jalan Kilang-Timor, Singapore 0315

Lifestream
Nottingham, England

Rhema Ministries Trading
Randburg, South Africa

Salvation Book Centre
Petaling, Jaya, Malaysia

Successful Christian Living
Capetown, Rep. of South Africa

Vision Resources
Ponsonby, Auckland, New Zealand

WA Buchanan Company
Geebung, Queensland, Australia

Word Alive
Niverville, Manitoba, Canada

Inside the U.S., call toll free to order:
1-800-722-6774

Dedication

In loving memory of my father, Sam Wright, Sr., who loved me past his own pain; who while painfully accepting his past, encouraged me to press past something called "average"; who released me to be called "individual," and taught me the value of making a difference.

Dad, I'm trying.

Contents

Foreword

Often there arises a cry from the trenches of our society; a cry that is muffled by the ills that have perpetuated the distress from the beginning. We have become strangely deaf to the screaming realities of our emotional, spiritual, and relational dysfunction. Locked beneath our ever-growing egos and intense need for achievement is a building turmoil that is of gargantuan proportions. There is a longing in the heart of most men to discover themselves. We have discovered technology, we have evaluated history, we have challenged theology, but unfortunately we have neither discovered, evaluated, or challenged the mission field of the masculine heart. How shrill the bleeding trumpet that announces to us, "The plan of the Lord is to restore His army and strengthen His men." In addition, there is a real need for us to come into a new-kindled awareness of who we are and to Whom we are committed.

No accomplishment will satisfy the inner thirst that constantly reminds wise men that all other pursuits are vanity and of little profit. From the lofty skylines of New York City to the sun-drenched asphalt jungles of Los Angeles, there is an ever-growing need for men to become comfortable with themselves and their God-given purpose and goals. Our families are literally decomposing as our relationships are being laid waste by stress. Worse still is the reality that our failing relationships are merely the side effects of our inner discontentment within ourselves. It is impossible to give in a relationship what you have not yourself received. Ultimately, we can only give to others what was given to us. If there is no deposit, there can be no withdrawal.

The great concern lies in the hearts of men who are constantly faced with withdrawal slips presented either by their wives, children, or professions. There seems to be a greater demand placed upon us than we have been supplied. When we become overdrawn, our insufficiency can become a spawning bed for angers, obsessions, and perversions. Futile attempts have been made by many men to regulate the demands of life. This is futile because we cannot stop people from needing whatever they need. The need remains unaltered regardless of our complaining. Those persons and places that make up our environment still approach us in deep anticipation, expecting more from us than we have received from those to whom we have looked.

Hear my cry O, God; attend unto my prayer. From the end of the earth will I cry unto thee, when my heart is overwhelmed: lead me to the rock that is higher than I. For thou hast been a shelter for me, and a strong tower from the enemy (Psalm 61:1-3).

Only God's graces can balance a heart that is overwhelmed. It is in distress that we reach outside of our societies and systems and cry out to the invincible power of God to strengthen the breaches in our own character and persona. The real challenge is to break the silence of the masculine heart, whose silence often becomes a sign of consent that allows the enemy to release his choice assasins upon us. We are dying silently—some in business suits, some in jogging suits. Regardless of the specificity of our life style, there is a cold war that has assaulted the masculine heart. If the silence could be broken, then like David, we would cry out. If we could lay down our armour and allow the fatherly affection of a sensitive God to reaffirm the little boy that hides within us all, we could survive.

As Dr. Wright takes us on a voyage to the bottom of our own hearts and airs out the dank, dark secrets of unresolved issues, we can't help but be forever changed by the greatness of God's wisdom. The thing that separates the child molester from the child nurturer is not the touch alone, but the intent of the touch. It is amazing that the same hand can touch the same person, but depending on the intent of the touch, the effect is completely different. Men all over this country are looking diligently for answers to old issues. We don't want to be fondled; we want to be nurtured. Many authors have tackled this subject, but their words didn't nurture us, they only molested what life had already abused.

Finally, we have a clear word that challenges us without emasculating us. The intent can be felt as God touches sensitive issues without violating valued principles. Only the hand of a whole father can touch a fragmented child and leave him *better* and not *bitter*. It has been a long night for men; we have been thrown overboard like Jonah into the cold deep of inner conflict. Our rebellion against God has led to confusion about ourselves. From male bashing to role reversal, we have been tossed to and fro on an angry sea; desperate, distraught litle boys hide behind our strong masculine frames—the body has grown, but the wrestling match hides behind our facade. Yes, little boys are all dressed up in men's bodies. We fight to get the person on the inside to develop simultaneously with the person on the outside. Do we bury our childhood issues beneath our adult succes? Or is it possible to resolve the conflicts that stop us from enjoying adulthood?

Hearken to my voice, my sister, and attend to my cry. Every woman needs to look at this insightful report, as most men have been engrossed in a fight to which most of our mothers, wives, and sisters are oblivious. There is a need to understand us even if you can't correct us. We can only confront the perils of our night if the women in our lives would understand the terror that blocks most men from the light of wholesome relationships and naked communication. The only solution lies in a need we have to confront what has not been corrected. If there is a helpmeet in this world, then let her *help meet* the needs of the struggling prince who thinks himself less than what he was created to be. In the process of cheering and praying for the "wrestler" whose ring is locked in the ropes of his own mind, you will see that our needs are unique, but not different.

Finally, I am so excited to have this opportunity to embrace issues that have previously been ignored. We have been called for such a time as this. Every man who has the courage to attack this precious text will find himself training for the fight with all the agility of mind that can be humanly achieved. Where most men train through clanging weights and sweat-drenched exercise, we train through the teary eyes of dreaming men who have been awakened to the call of God. Yes sir, wake up; we are in a fight! But we are going to win! We have been through the test and the struggles. We have played the game and avoided the issues. But "tonight," O enemy of mine, "tonight," O memory of mine, you've climbed in this ring with someone who means business! By the time the referee rings the bell, it will be apparent that the men of this century are ready to do battle. So come what will, and work what may—our running is over! No sissified backing up, and no running home to "Momma"; *Tonight, We Wrestle.*

Bishop T.D. Jakes
Assistant Presiding Prelate
Higher Ground Assemblies
Pastor, Temple of Faith Ministries
Charleston, WV

Preface

On a fair Sunday morning in May 1987, the Lord's presence in me suggested warmly that the morning worship service would be different somehow. This day was sure to bring a specially tailored blessing just for me. As the order of the worship service became progressively more involved, I became more reverently aware of the fact that the Father was present to do more than just receive our praise. By the time the choir began to minister, I felt a compelling unction to re-engage in worship before the Lord. I didn't resist. In just a few seconds, something phenomenal began to take place around me in the spirit realm. Suddenly, the refreshing splendor of the Lord's presence in the room swept across the pulpit platform area where I was seated. It generated a gravitational pull so strong that it felt as if I were being lifted some two feet above the platform and ushered down the center isles—all the way out of the front doors onto the church grounds. As I recall this is where the chair, with me seated in it, came to a halt.

At this point of my experience, my eyes beheld something startling. The sight caused me to rise to my feet in awe; I saw a multitude of anonymous individuals. Actually "a multitude" is an understatement. There were so many that I could not see the other side of the street. They were standing literally jammed together shoulder to shoulder; there was no room for them to move. Never had I witnessed such a large mass of people in one place, especially outside of a church, without their attention focused on an apparent popular outdoors event.

I was anxious to figure out the meaning and receive the fullness of this vision; I asked myself, "Who are these people, and from whence have they come?" After all, these people were neither black nor white; they were grey. They were neither young nor old. They were neither men nor women, boys nor girls. My anxiety soon turned into wonder. I tried to gaze and guess at their number, but as I continued to look from my right to my left to see where their numbers stopped, the crowd appeared to be so great that there didn't seem to be an end to it at all. They were scattered all the way to the end of my sight. It was fascinating!

At this time, I decided to inquire of the Lord the question I had asked myself, not knowing that the answer would change me for life. I asked Him, "Who are these people and from whence have they come?" Without hesitation, the Father replied with one of the most painful answers I have ever received. "These are they," He said, "that have been wounded in the House of God!"

I remember being overwhelmed. I also remember wondering out loud, "Has the Body of Christ been guilty of being insensitive, uncaring, and self-serving? Moreover, have I myself been guilty of inflicting wounds upon God's people? Has my denominational affiliation or organizational ambition caused me to possess or show a false sense of superiority?" Before I could reflect upon this any further or answer myself, I found myself back in the pulpit in the midst of worship. I knelt sorrowfully before the Father asking in earnest how this mass of wounded souls could be helped.

When I came to myself, my face was disfigured from empathy for the concentrated pain within the hearts of all of "these" who had stood in the streets. I remember looking out into my congregation. I asked if there were any among us who felt that they were being overlooked. Then the Father gently made a request of my life that has changed me to this day. He said, "Son, go after them. Show them My love. I died for them. I love them, for they are Mine. Bring them home."

To those of you who are wounded, who feel alone and left out of a religion that offers no answers, it is with great joy that I can now speak strength and encouragement into your life by sharing this truth: The Father is waiting with His arms open wide to envelope you into an enlightening, fulfilling relationship with Him.

My prayer is that whatever has hurt you, whomever it was that disappointed you, however small, unimportant, unneeded, or unappreciated you were made to feel, or however you have been placed into a life-depressing dilemma, the situation might be resolved conclusively by allowing His Holy presence to bring you home safely.

Dr. Donald A. Wright

Assignment of Identity: The Paternal Predictor

Chapter One

Who Am I?

One of the greatest tragedies of life is to run head first into yourself. In a world brimming with cellular car phones, automatic cash tellers, and touchtone fax machines, who would think that such a thing could ever happen? Despite the thoughts on the issue, tragedies can be prevented. The key rests upon recognizing the symptoms. Even in the darkness of subconscious behavior, God's abundant mercies still protect His children from the calamity of being "utterly cast down." The heavenly Father has stepped into this season to triumphantly rescue us, His sons and daughters, from the ills that flesh is heir to, ills from which we could not rescue ourselves. That is why we worship Him with the passion that we do; we couldn't do it by ourselves.

Often I think of how life could have been. Worse, I think of how it almost was. Each time I conclude a session of one-on-one witnessing, individual counseling, or public ministering, I deliberately reflect upon how the love of God has maximized the expression "crisis intervention." The heavenly Father's intervention became a reality the day I looked out into the pasture of the Christian brotherhood and observed worship, fellowship, and years of service bound within a cage labeled "Who am I?"

After office hours one weekend, I flipped tiredly through the pages of my personal journal of case notes. While rubbing my book-sore eyes like a child fighting sleep, a demographical pattern presented itself to me. A basic doubt was lodged in the hearts of some of our faithful brothers.

Though they were in pursuit of Christian directions for their lives, they were urgently seeking explanations that would be psychologically convincing. Most were unfathered (or barely fathered) men, loyal servants in the Body of Christ, and those who were not divorced from their wives were in danger of being divorced from themselves. The sadly spoken utterance of the three words "Who am I?" were equally as sensitive in their expression and tone as the three words, "I miss Dad."

There was no doubt that modern techniques for counseling were being faced with a critical reality. The reality was that after man has first faced himself and learned himself, there is yet a final struggle of needing to live peacefully with himself. Personality inventories were producing questions of their own. Interestingly, the question of identity was being asked by twice as many men as women. The equally urgent issues that belong to God's premiere creation—man—are emerging with loud demands. These issues are primarily involved with man's need to talk about in his relationship with God that which he has been afraid to mention ever since he discovered something was missing. Regardless of gender, this phenomena is critical because the prevailing influence of the Creator has not been rightfully included in the overall analysis of self.

I am convinced that psychology and theology occasionally intersect at the crossroads of life—for the good of the individual—even though the two areas of study have evolved from different worlds. When they meet face to face, for the purpose of sorting out the issues of life, they agree that the total spirit, soul, and body of man should benefit from their combined, but never compromised, disciplines. However, when the question resounds, "Who am I?" basic theology stands apart in this respect: When man became a living soul, his human existence was shaped into the image of God for the purpose of worship, fellowship, and enjoying God's pleasures forever.

Man can miss out on such a fulfilling worship experience if he does not first view himself as being made in the image of God, and from the Father's projection, assume his own true identity. This is a delicate area of Christianity. It is in essence, where the inner struggle for self-identity either triumphs or succumbs to spiritual fluster. Having said that, there emerges a need for recovery.

There's nothing new about this phenomenon. In the Word of God, we are led through the saga of man's battles, relationships, struggles, and disappointments. After studying the life patterns of the Israelites, their descendants, and the early Church, we have been brought through our studies back to the truth that man was created to experience *peaceful* fellowship with God. Mankind at large faces an *unpeaceful* dilemma because man so desperately needs an exodus or "deliverance" from the bondage of not fully knowing *who he is*. Indeed, man is a living soul, but still there is the chance that his senses have been damaged by the taste of poor self concepts.

We are finally learning as men how to trace the path of this epidemic; however, only the Spirit of God can settle this discrepancy that can consequently stunt our growth, handicap our whole manhood, and inhibit our worship. Thus, the impassioned concern of this text is that our streets, pilot seats, engineering seats, pulpit seats, and even our seats on Capitol Hill are at risk of being filled with "too many boys" and not enough "men." For definition, the term *boy* is used respectably here to refer to a man whose behavior reflects the need for recovery from having been neglected, abused, or rejected during his childhood. The consequence of which is that he may not have fully grown up nor matured in his walk with God.

As it also happens, we would be remiss to disregard the fact that there are women whose female maturity in Christ has never been conclusively confirmed because she too has never been acknowledged as such by a significant or inspiring role model. Therefore, her destiny as a missionary, evangelist, teacher, and mother is fractured. In either or both cases, there is a need for recovery.

Unfortunately, the term *recovery* often frightens those whose relationship with God is the only strand of hope between turning to alternative life styles and completely giving up. Without harping upon theological dogmatics, the focus of this message is to guide men and women with fractured identities to a face-to-face encounter with the almighty wonderful Counselor. With all due respect to the prominence of psychoanalytic treatment, in the face of total deliverance, it is sadly limited. In the end, its methods cannot do *analytically* what theology can do *completely*.

The purpose of counseling is to provide insight and relief through a clear understanding of oneself in the context of crisis. The aim of ministry is to provide enduring treatment for long-imbedded problems with complete victory and deliverance as the final goal. Although both subscribe to the methodology of measuring one's own sense of identity, ministry's active agent is conducted through the vehicle of faith.

Such an attitude is built upon the hope of obtaining distinct answers even where no apparent evidence is seen (see Heb. 11:1). It is our functional faith that says, "I don't believe this struggle to find myself should be a lifelong process. I believe there is a God-given solution." This statement of faith accurately attributes credit to the heavenly Father as being the only authority who will provide absolute truth in answer to the repeated question, "Who am I?" According to the great work that has begun in us, *who we are,* as you will conclude through the following discussions, case studies, and behavioral observations, is only a part (but nevertheless the core) of who we are *destined to become* in God. Once our excellent personal calling and purpose in God is "made sure," we can fully avail ourselves in worship to be consecrated, equipped, and thoroughly furnished as men of God unto every good and perfect work (see 2 Tim. 3:17).

Unlike psychology, theology bases its method of "recovery" upon complete salvation and deliverance—and in this case, divine insight. This insight into everyday human life will reveal to us the underrated strength of human influence. As the superior species, the human race indirectly influences the behavior of all other species. This also serves as genuine proof that a single human's influence upon another has the kind of impact that can be observed over a lifetime. Whether the influence is positive or negative, peaceful or confusing, the impact endures. Consequently the impact of *mistaken identity* can seem to take a lifetime to correct.

The aim pinpointed here is that in the absence of peace and in the presence of confusion, we must resolve that this unplanned predicament of mistaken indentity has not come from the Creator (see 1 Cor. 14:33). When confusion abounds and we begin to compare ourselves with ourselves, the resulting question is "Who am I?" How do we respond? Some respond, "I am a respected Sunday school teacher" or "I am an entrepreneur with a flourishing business." Others respond, "I am a gifted psalmist who has moved entire assemblies to the point of tears through my delivery of the song ministry."

However, if the intimate truth were to be known, and if we were to take a moment to consider the possible barrier between ourselves and the Lord God, many of us would admit, "I am struggling through crisis after crisis because my walk with God is not what it should be. I am hurting, I am a stranger to myself, and I am tired. My Christianity seems to be stagnant because of what I believe happened while I was too young to be held responsible for anything. There are experiences that have intruded painfully upon my once innocent concept of what a true man is. But it happened so long ago that I never thought I would feel the pains of it in my Christian career."

Beloved, something has happened in our hearts that our blessed Creator has not endorsed: Our hearts have been broken. But there is a mending for our brokenness if we will but trust Him with the broken pieces.

At long last, my brothers, I have been released by the Father to pass on to you this revelation as it was imparted to me after a season of distress-provoked questions and sleepless nights. Listen carefully: A confrontation took place in the Scriptures. The confrontation marked a night of soul-searching. Tonight it's going to happen all over again regardless of what hour of the night your life is in. This evening, God unlocks closed issues and asks, "Where did it all begin? Do you remember where you were first sidetracked from becoming all that you should? Who gave you (or robbed you of) your sense of self-worth? Who gave you your identity? Who was it that intimidated you with that cold, brisk answer to your truehearted questions as a child? Who caused you to be afraid to explore the truth of your God?" Why are we afraid to examine the truth of ourselves and of our home environment? Who was it that spoiled your early walk with the Lord by mocking your sincerity? The Father wants to know who it was that made you afraid to fully express yourself and caused you to miss out on really getting to know yourself. Who gave you a name that left you wanting self-certainty? Who named you? What were the first words spoken over your life? The Father wants you to know that you can talk about it now.

In the Bible, names usually hold a symbolic meaning, and often they depict the very character of the person named, as in the case of Jacob, son of Isaac (Gen. 27:36). Brother Jacob will serve as our principle example throughout these guidelines for climbing over the walls of despair. Jacob's life, complicated by abuse, rejection, neglect, and early childhood labeling, was delivered of these complications when, at last, the Lord met him in the night and carried him back into the most difficult experiences of his childhood. His father had shamelessly named him "Trickster"; and in his struggles to find himself, he succeeded in living up to the title.

God wants to take us back to that initial experience that left an emotional scar upon us. Jacob's scar had been carved into him by the strongest human figure in his life. Notice the many pains Jacob went through in Genesis 25–33 just to receive the blessing of the person in his life whose opinion, criticism, and authority meant the most—His father Isaac.

Tonight, the *Jacob* that is possibly present in each of us will realize that his father's opinion had kept him bound in a cage of fear and craving for approval since childhood. Tonight we, like Jacob, are destined to meet God, to let go, and to allow the truth within us to come out. We too must painfully revisit the past, if only to learn that God has been waiting all this time to heal us and confirm our truthful identity. In your private hours of prayer and meditation, has the cause for your unstable walk with God ever been cross-examined? Has anyone ever taken the time to explain to you the difference between a *lame walk in God* and a *limping walk with God*, and the blessed, permanent significance of the latter? Has your eagerness for the constant approval of others ever been shelved for a few moments to consider the opinion of Christ? Have you wondered lately what Christ's honest opinion is of what you have done with your life since you accepted Him as your Savior? We might begin our own self-analysis in searching the mind of Christ by conveying the virtue of honesty as joint heirs of His personality. Who does *He* say we are?

Christ's sure hope that we would be successful in living up to the favor of being called by His name is an honor that makes our personal adoption a cut above the rest. The responsibility of assigning our identity to us, His descendants, was passed onto His disciples. Some 65 years after Christ went away, one of them—namely Peter—blessed us with the character name "peculiar" (1 Pet. 2:9).

What is Christ's opinion of how we have anxiously tried to be the exact opposite of *peculiar*? Because the world pokes fun at the term *peculiar* we have permitted this unpopularity to pronounce our identity in this life. How then shall Christ recognize us—His people—by name when He returns if we have given in to the opinions of those that matter least? The Jacobic history repeats itself. How do you suppose Christ feels about that?

We, the people of God, like the restored and renamed Jacob, are protected with a covering of the Father's love that empowers us to withstand the storms of life. Through which, we are "troubled on every side, yet not in despair" (2 Cor. 4:8). Nevertheless, we are caught in a turbulent bind and cannot get out because we are crippled in our exercise of diligence to figure out *who we really are* (see 2 Pet. 1:10). We're not quite sure. We're not certain if we are truly the servants of the Kingdom that we were called to be, nor are we sure that we have become the witnesses that we have been charged to be. Our contributions to the ministry *are not* providing treatment for the human soul because we need to be spiritually treated ourselves. Even our worship experience is approached with heaviness. Instead of offering a true sacrifice of praise, we lift our hands with a superficial offering and

open our mouths with a plastic praise
"Who *am* I, anyway?" This battle from

Here in the midst of the battle, we
prophetic forecast, nor do we stand ii
wilderness retreat. What we need is a
from the Lord for deliverance. But how d ₋₋₋ₐᵤ happen?
"As a man thinketh in his heart, so is he" (see Prov. 23:7).
The issue is: What has man been taught to think he is? In
the course of treatment for overcoming poor character
labeling, psychological methods employ the concept of
"mind over matter." Theological treatment represents the
compassion of God that places "matter over mind," and the
question He then asks is, "What's the matter?"

The matter in paternal prediction (individual character
and personality as determined by Dad) and assignment of
identity has little to do with the the chromosomal sampling
that serves to determine your sex and features, and even
less to do with the unpopular ring that your name may
have. Quite often, however, it could have everything to do
with your reaction to what your name actually means. That
being the case, man's thinking and behavior is likely to
take on the sum and substance of his name.

How do the facts from your past add up for you? There
may be those who feel the issue is being raised after the fact,
and that "what's done is done" and cannot be changed. My assignment from the Father, however, is not to withdraw the
question for any reason, but to help bring to the surface the
underlying issue by challenging you to ponder why and how
you received your name. For example, were you named out of
the anxieties that come with new (or unplanned) parenthood?
Or were you perhaps named out of the possible controversy
that surrounded your conception? What (or who) does the
sound of your name remind your parents of? Does it remind
them of something (or someone) special? If so, have you been
treated special? Maybe it reminds them of something that

...y doesn't matter one way or the other. Have you been treated as though you don't matter? That's the *matter*.

This is a sensitive concern of paternal prediction and the parent-child relationship that results mainly because the power of determination, variation, and confirmation of identity has biologically come from the male parent. During conception the composotion of a child's blood is transferred from the father. The experimental labeling of human blood type as being either positive or negative becomes ironically thought-provoking. Temperamentally, a misidentified or unidentified man's own deep-rooted woe, "bad blood," and unanswered questions often bring with them hot-tempered bitterness and hostility to the bassinet of his newborn responsibility. The younger the child, the more innocently sensitive he is to these feelings which, at such a tender stage, may be experienced as rejection. These sour grapes, in turn, have been fed to children throughout the world of Christianity. Today, we as the generation that has survived these unsavory drops straight from the grapevine are tense, uptight, and our teeth are set on edge (see Ezek. 18:2). That's the matter.

What is more of the matter is that *unidentified* sons grow up to become fathers who will typically still possess the kind of power and influence over their children that will make a lifelong impression. Those impressions when void of fatherly confirmation, are manifested as just that—impressions—and the child, as early as he can control his behavior becomes motivated by public opinion. Now that he has grown up, the adult "boy" is still driven by public opinion rather than divine purpose. It is arresting to notice how closely we compare with Jacob. Are there any lengths that we would not go to simply to win the affection, approval, acceptance, and attention of our father? (See Genesis 24–27.) In Jacob's life, the pattern served only to create a stressful Christian atmosphere. Being forced out of the house to avoid conflict, matching deceit with more deceit,

and literally gambling with another's blessing painted a behavioral cycle that sooner or later echoed an emotional cry
more painful than the agony of physical abuse. Suppressed
feelings of failure are naturally revealed in our cry when
we stand at the altar. And in search for a quick post-altar
call remedy, we shuffle through the crowd seeking other
avenues of approval. Evidently, the root of our feelings of
failure are never admitted or released when we cry out to
the Lord at the altar.

For the man who has laid his tensions at the altar but
has not released the source, God desires to mightily destroy
the yoke of fear and failure from upon you so that it does
not go into recession, but into oblivion. Christ has not given
us a compulsive drive for success nor has He piloted us
toward failure. He only says, "believe."

Like public opinion, success on any level has a way of
nudging man to admire his own accomplishments and
place him in touch with an exalted concept of who he is.
The problem is that all too often these victories fall under
false pretense. Social status, employment, even church affiliation all offer a sense of belonging, but they rob us of the
same with feelings of misplacement, if by chance we are
removed from them. Social status declines overnight. Ca-
reers come and go. Neither of these hold any eternal value.
On that account, is it not valid to insist that a functional
place in God's perfect will outweighs the elastic strength of
the self-fulfillment found in climbing the ranks of the organizational world? These self-styled measures of success
are only a distinctive portion of the larger whole of *who we
really are.* Searching for the root of this kind of thinking
will lead man back to early household and social experiences. He will soon discover that these false measures may
have been channeled through parental bonding (or lack of
bonding, as the case may be), sibling rivalry, extended
family relationships or even the absence of proper guidance
during the early and vital formative years. Whatever the
case, the true believer will defend God's lovingkindness and

uphold the certainty that these influences have not come from the Father.

In the occasional emptiness of the adult male's personal power, he starts searching for privileges. When the searching heart of man accepts the privilege to communicate this long-imbedded discrepancy in his spirit to the heavenly Father, he will have taken the first step toward acquiring an understanding of who he is truly meant to be. He will learn that he is not meant to be abused, rejected, or identified by any name less distinguished than *Hephzibah* (Is. 62:4). Yes, as the adoptive son of the heavenly Father, you have every right to be called "My pleasure, My valuable one, My acceptable, delightful, pleasant purpose" *Heph-zibah*. There's relieving affection in this definition of our privileged name in the kingdom. There is relief in this genuine Father-son relationship between God and those who believe on *His* name (see Jn. 1:12). You are the sons of God, not by a mere claim or desperate interest, but by actual generation; you are the legitimate offspring of God Himself! The reality that this relationship brings to light cannot be overstated. Our merge into the Father's holiness substantiates our kindred identity. (See 2 Corinthians 6:17-18.)

On the other hand, unfitting names hurt and embarrass us. We shield ourselves from this embarrassment behind a false outward expression. We wear masks throughout life and die having *never* reached our potential in Christ. Our lives are destined to a marvelous calling that cannot endure the sting of misidentification beyond this point. Tearful, ashamed Christians will rid themselves of their needless self-blame when the Father lifts the blame from them and hides them behind the cross for as long as it takes for them to recuperate. The length of time for recuperation is not important. What's important is that we have been delivered the promise that we shall surely survive the surgery. Once tucked safely behind the protective cover of the cross, we can remove our masks, face ourselves, stand nakedly honest before our Creator and claim back our birthright—our name—our identity. In fact, you will not get any rest *tonight* until you are free of any and every self-doubt, and are able with abundant joy to bring forth a glad praise in the earth (Is. 62:7)!

Let us survey the theological analysis of paternal prediction and assignment of identity as it was applied to the disciple who was more than a first cousin to Christ, but was one of His closest brothers and fondest friends: John the Baptist. Inasmuch as John knew that he was a man "sent by God" (Jn. 1:6), he had a solid enough grip on his identity, so that 13 verses later, when he was asked "Who art thou?" he immediately made it know who he *was not*. He knew his name. He knew his purpose. And he knew the extent of his ministry. He affirmed,

> *There standeth one among you, whom ye know not;*
> *He it is, who coming after me, whose shoe's latchet I*
> *am not worthy to unloose* (John 1:26b-27).

Listen to the first words spoken over him by his father, Zacharias at his birth:

> *And thou, child, shalt be called the prophet of the*
> *Highest: for thou shalt go before the face of the Lord*
> *to prepare His ways; to give knowledge of salvation*
> *unto His people by the remission of their sins* (Luke
> 1:76-77).

How was John's destiny and life affected by this announcement spoken directly into his life?

> *...the child grew, and waxed strong in spirit, and*
> *was in the deserts till the day of his shewing unto Is-*
> *rael* (Luke 1:80).

Here you have it, the heart of the analysis; John was destined to be called by a name that was synonymous with success in the work of the Lord (and so are you). In fact, on the day of John's circumcision, God did not allow Zacharias to speak until he called his son by his proper name "John" (Lk. 1:63-64). Wouldn't it be a milestone in true manhood if we as men were to name our children what God would want them to be named? Yet our children are being baptized with names that God did not give us to name them.

Now in the life of Jacob, examine the practical contrast offered to the parent-child identity analysis: The first words by which Isaac identified his son were manifestly negative in nature; "and his name was called Jacob" (Gen. 25:26b). As insulting a name as that may sound, is it no wonder that the very first words recorded of Jacob, as spoken to his twin brother are: "Sell me this day thy birthright" (Gen. 25:31).

How accurately matched are his name and his character. But who put this crown of thorns upon him? Who named him "Jacob" in the first place? Who named us? Who spoke from our past and affected our present? Last night we nearly drowned in our past, but tonight we wrestle for our future.

God is infinitely wise of the possibility that perhaps there were words, names, innocent parental remarks over your life that prophesied that you would be "just like your father" or "You won't finish college." Could it be that there was a forecast stating, "You'll probably make a foolish mistake before marriage and embarrass the family." What was expected of you early in life? Did you fulfill those expectations? Honestly, who was the first person to say, "I told you so"? (Consider Genesis 27:35-36.) What did these words and names do to you? Has it caused you to nervously fidget with who you are? Tonight God is calling us to stop wiggling, to be still, and to know that He is God (see Ps. 46:10).

In contemplation of these thoughts from our past, one of the lessons of faith we are taught to apply to our lives, especially when we become parents ourselves, is that parenthood is an awesome responsibility. In the absence of the current over-extended sociological advice for parenting existing since the 1960's, we can safely conclude that our own mothers and fathers apparently did their very best to breed us into a normal, healthy, happy, godly life style. However, if their own personal life stories have been haunted by leftover disappointments and conflicts, who have they fed the leftovers to? Blessed be tonight's appointment with the power of God that will invite us to make up for any lost time and soothe the bitter taste of any stale leftover emotions. Tonight, less time will be spent compromising our walk in the center of God's will to achieve the relief and satisfaction of making our parents proud; more time will be spent submitting to the purpose that was ordained for our life while we were yet in the womb.

While the evening approaches, pewfuls of us are wandering through a maze in our Christian walk. Year after year, week after week, it is becoming essentially impossible for us to draw any water for fruitful living from the wells of salvation because we are deplete of real joy. From coast to coast, whether in the billion-dollar cathedral, or in the inner-city storefront—holy sanctuaries are overloaded with wall-to-wall worshipers who were never handled with the kind of human lovingkindness that reinforces God's love; and because no one ever blessed our lives and made us feel special, we fail to bless God! The Christian life will linger on pitifully and be left destitute of blessings whenever we default in rendering unto God due praise. A short-circuited worship experience—void of spiritual electricity and incapable of soaring to a higher plane—only further frustrates the whole picture. We then find ourselves bitter and threatened with a negative outlook on life. How is it that we cannot see ourselves in the Most Holy Place before God after nearly a lifetime of acknowledging Him as our

Lord? Where did these feelings of inferiority and inadequacy evolve that debate over whether or not that we even belong in such a holy realm that takes us "out of this world"? Who told us that we are not superior to the heathen personalities of the land? Surely the Holy Ghost has not suggested such a thing. Something within us has been shaped improperly, and has caused us to walk, think, and live as Kingdom builders with insufficient tools.

Our works in the Kingdom are only as meaningful in God's eyes as our personal worth is in our own eyes. Secondhand viewpoints such as criticism (in excess) have become a damaging trend that tests our self-opinion against that of others. And because it is usually unsolicited, the fact that it is merely what is seen through the eyes of others should only make it, at most, the last of our concerns. We owe it to ourselves to see to it that this trend discontinues by tactfully rebuking the oncoming signals, for it holds no relevancy to man's relationship with his Creator.

I submit that criticism, which can seem most negative in childhood, should end with the positive opposite of what is being criticized and be measured by the standards of the gospel. With Christ as the universal standard of truth, we may look to Him listen to His opinion, bond with Him, experience the impartation of His image in us, and grasp hold of *who we really are.* No longer should the brotherhood look through the eyes of others and ask, *"Who am I?"* and in the same breath ponder, *"Where did I go wrong?"* Well, it's not that simple. Something "went wrong" in this light not long after Adam's error in the Garden of Eden. Thus, the challenge presented through this backtracked promise of healing is focused less on *"Where did you go wrong?"* and more on *"Will you arise and break the curse?"*

Considering the fact that "God will surely visit you" as early as tonight (see Gen. 50:25), it is especially important for we as men to stand as solid as steel so that together, we might confidently confirm the working of all things "...together for the good to them that love God, to them who are the called according to His purpose" (Rom. 8:28). And if by chance your heart is grieved with the idea that nobody understands the pain you feel, the peace of God as your remedy of treatment will pass "all understanding" (see Phil. 4:7). The Scripture is clear that "the Lord is at hand" and that once man's deep concerns are "made known unto God" his true self will be revealed and his healing will be sealed through Him. (See Philippians 4:5-6.)

As I tuck away the joys of this final solution for a few chapters, I am brought back to the question at hand. Have you ever silently asked yourself *"Who am I?"* Come stand behind this translucent glass and look upon mankind with me; it is weeping and disguised. It is weeping because it is hurting. It is disguised because it is scarred. I see towering executives, on the verge of divorce, alcoholism, and backsliding, masked in disguise by the phony boast of corporate success. I see construction workers masked like mannequins, their unbearable hurt cleverly hidden behind industrial toughness. When it comes to our feelings we "hide" but never "go seek." Educational psychology will concur that learned behavior, such as pretending, is maintained over extended periods. It therefore requires long-term examination. Clinical therapy, however, is inefficient to cut treatment down to a six-hour struggle and then kiss the restored sufferer with a new identity. Only God can speak over and into our lives and between "sundown" and "sunup" reassign our identity. "Thy name shall be called no more Jacob" ...*no more Jacob...no more*—listen to the restorative sound of this pledge from the Father. (See Genesis 32:28.)

As the night approaches, you can breathe a sigh of relief that you will soon learn your rightful place in the congregation of the righteous. Prepare to walk away from behind this glass with everlasting joy, rejoicing and accurately recollecting the moment the Lord called you by a new name. If it's nothing short of a miracle that you need on tonight, the heavenly Father's ultimatum is now spoken to you to free you from your painful past. And should you choose to hide, struggle, or even conceal the truth about those situations that keep you out of touch with yourself, His hands will lovingly reach farther and farther into your past until your fragile frame is bent to full surrender— *tonight, we wrestle.*

It doesn't end there. Tonight we launch out into deep waters where burdens, yokes, and experiences that have been pushed into the back of your mind and forced to assume a low profile will be confronted and verbally ventilated. It doesn't end here because I, furthermore, see young men reaching past their fathers and establishing meaningful friendships with their grandfathers while their own fathers remain unhealed. Don't you see it also?

I see sisters in the Lord perplexed by feelings of inadequacy in their marriages because their gifts, callings, and purpose in the ministry have never been acknowledged by their fathers. Come stand a little closer to me. Notice where I'm pointing—over there—don't you recognize those dear brothers? They've been standing out on that street corner for years, wanting to reach out for the embrace of the preacher, but the preacher has his arms around himself, so as not to expose his own fears and inability to strengthen the brotherhood. I see wounded adult men who somehow got off to a bad start in life. They have only recently realized it and how it has hampered their progress in God. I see them perplexed by emptiness, loneliness, and many, many unanswered questions. If you look even closer, you will see that it is not the world of sin only that is buried in dilemma, but the body of believers in Christ. We too are the victims.

The first day of the best years of your life will begin the moment you set yourself free from the plagues of mankind.

That moment will occur tonight. Tonight, pour out to God the pain that was poured into you years ago. Nothing will matter tonight, except the truth. The mighty biblical men of valor's most heroic deeds came out of their inevitable moments of admitting to God the lineage of their failures.

In David's distress He pleaded with the Lord, "Cleanse thou me from secret faults [and fears and those unspeakable things that I dare not tell another]" (Ps. 19:12b). If I open my mouth just, "Let the words of my mouth, and the meditation of my heart, be acceptable in Thy sight, O Lord, my strength and my redeemer" (Ps. 19:14). Though from a dysfunctional family himself, David reflected upon the grace of God at work in his manhood and pondered the awesome thought "Who am I that God is even mindful of me. In the presumably doomed future that threatens my worship, I want to know who am I that He visiteth me and cares so much as to ask, 'What's the matter?' " (See Psalm 8:4.)

Inside of all this apprehension, still the Father asks, "What is the matter?" The matter is that many of us have never been properly touched as children, therefore we are confused as adults over the value of affection. The matter is our father's pain. The matter is our dormant salvation, our wounded spirits. The matter is that it seems that our cries for attention, approval, and acceptance have been blatantly disregarded. The matter is the embarrassing side effects of our emotionally imbalanced family units. Family matters, although ordinarily well-hidden (and not dared to be admitted), call for family ministry. From those isolated, still integrated, conflicts that often are complicated by the unsettled father figure, we have come to identify that men genuinely need other men for bonding. Fathers need their sons for the redemption of their own imperfections. Sons need fathers for confirmation of identity. Fathers need their fathers for transgenerational passage of values. Wives need their husbands for soul mates. And we *all* need Christ to turn to, whose precious blood alone will cover the spiritual-ly undesirable behavior associated with our suppressed un-happiness that ultimately admits, "*I have a need.*"

Because man's true comfort level with his true self is trapped behind the cell bars of public opinion, social suc-cess, and unconstructive criticism, and because the slight-est manlike expression of emotional sensitivity becomes self-incriminating, Jesus intervenes tonight and invites us to freely come toward Him. Jesus says to you today, "...lie your head down upon my breast, those of you whose iden-tity crises have become a heavy, weary burden. You will find rest for your soul by looking to Me and learning of Me. Observe My manly posture; I am meek and lowly of heart." (See Matthew 11:28-29.) Tonight, in so doing, the ambience of His Glory will shine around you for others to see. That's the key. We are destined to become "fishers of men" who will bring others into the Body to realize and experience real manhood through Christ. Somewhere deep inside we know that we are selectively privileged to be cradled day by day in Jehovah's complete care.

Until we face those things deep inside, the earthly father remains hurt and continues to subconsciously call his son by an old name. It is an old name because it is precisely what his father called him. As the child's per-sonality develops, the son (or daughter) who has been labeled remains scarred with wounds that often last a lifetime. But the heavenly Father awaits to call us by a new name and wash away the bitterness and frustration. It's a new name because it brings us face to face with the actual greatness we possess. It's a new name because we never knew (and certainly never believed) that we are great, chosen, royal, and anointed vessels for the Master's use and for the indwelling of His glory. From the moment we confess to the Father *how* we have been robbed of our divine birthright, "old things" are promised to pass away, a new self-identity will evolve, a sturdier human temple will be built, a more secure personality will be planted, and the enslaved prince (and princess) in us will be set free; and whom the Son makes free, is free indeed (See Jn. 8:36). This is the prelude to—Praise God—a *solved mystery.*

Tonight it is no longer mysterious that psychology at its best is limited to merely surmising *who we think we are.* Whereas theology, the rightly divided prescription of every word that proceeds out of the mouth of God, brings out our true and predestined identity by feeding the spirit man with diving truths. As a science, theology shovels out the surface residue of reason and logic, digs up the pent-up emotions, examines man's properties, reaffirms his meaning, substantiates his purpose, cures his bitterness, carves into him a new name, and calls him by the name that denotes *who he is meant to become*—influence, purpose, destiny, identity.

In case you got stuck on the question, "Who named you?" several paragraphs back and you can't seem to focus upon anything else, I pray that you will keenly hear the heartbeat of this dispensation, not as a subtle attack intended to unfairly assign blame where it does not belong, but a message of self-understanding, deliverance, and love issued forth from the throne of God. It is shared so that we might be blessed through knowing that *who we are* is the "alpha and omega" of issues that we must face close-up, if we are to understand how and where we are to fit into relationship with our God. We know that fathers do not intentionally sow wounds into their children's lives. Psychology and sociology have not conveyed to man the power and pattern of his own influence. He has not been shown the total picture of how his natural strength, both verbal and emotional, effectuate change in the lives of others. Only the work of God can show this to him in the way he needs to see it. And tonight, fatherless sons, fatherless fathers, bruised brothers (and sisters), all those who hurt, as you read on, I challenge you in the name of Jesus to take the first step toward letting it go, and say, "Yes, Lord, it's me. It has taken me years to admit that I really don't know exactly *who I am* but as of this very moment, I passionately desire to become the man You have created and called me to be...and I won't let go until You make me into that real man!"

How gloriously refreshing it is to commune in the following pages with the idea that in these last days, young men's visions *will* come to pass, and that old men's dreams really do come true! (See Joel 2:28.)

**Roles, Molds,
and Strongholds**

Chapter Two

Who Made Me This Way?

What would you suppose has the longest lifespan in a boy's treasure chest? An autographed Chicago White Sox catcher's mit, maybe a Cub Scout's honor badge, or perhaps a personalized souvenir from his favorite movie hero? Or how about a spiritually and emotionally committed Dad who is reachable enough to help make his boyhood complete by steering his young feet toward an undefeated, Christ-centered walk through life? Our prized possessions—our sons—are waiting in the wings of the home for something to happen. They don't *expect* much, but they *want* as much out of us as we can give. This includes finding a way to share with them the exhanged father-son conversation that we perhaps may not have experienced as children, while offering them *nothing less* than what God has shared with us as adults. The infinitely important role of the father has been underscored in an increasing number of psychological studies that conclude it is the father who is the primary influence regarding sex roles for both boys and girls. It can be safely said that the father not only calls for masculinity in boys, but feminity in girls as well. Interwoven into the brilliance of Solomon's wisdom for building relationships and Paul's gift for church and family administration, the Scriptures have respectfully suggested that the expectations of Dad in son and daughter conditioning are noble; and may even prove to be his unsung calling.

Part of this historic calling is to help his child discover who and what it is that God means him to be and do. Parents must train up children, not simply in the way that any and every child should go, but also in the specific and unique way in which that child should go. These appointed paths are determined by the seed of talent the child individually possesses. As a rule to follow, once this process begins, remember; it is the heavenly Father who creates and gives the seed, the earthly father plants and nourishes it, and when the Spirit of the Lord blows upon it, it grows. The Lord commands us as parents to exercise love, discipline, and instruction in fulfilling our calling. Carefully handling, shaping, and seasoning our children's personalities in the fear and reverence of God is our reasonable service. These three duties involve helping the child to cultivate an awareness of his or her unique place and function in the Body of Christ and in the home. To "train" a child, therefore, is to instill appropriate values. To "train up" a child is to prayerfully realize, unveil, and stir-up his personal anointing from childhood to early adulthood. There is, indeed, a difference between the two terms. As it happens, both hold an individual significance in parenting that needs to be understood by both the parent and the child. What God has placed in your offspring is so unique, that *no man* is fit to give your child a name unless he first seeks God.

We, as parents, (especially fathers), must assume the privilege to be to our children what Christ was among other men—a gentle example of truth governed by the mind of the Father. Discipline doesn't always have to be enforced with hostility, although it may be an approach that was familiar in your own upbringing. As male parents and as shepherds of our homes, we might also consider learning how to reasonably manipulate a "rodstaff." This involves taking hold of the top of the rod to embrace your sheep with love, yet using the staff to keep them close enough to you to let them know that you are there to keep them in line and maintain order—order patterned after the love of the Lord, who loves and corrects "even as a father the son in whom he delighteth" (Prov. 3:12b).

In want of explicit directions, modern fatherhood is asking in despair, "How do I affirm my son's masculinity and at the same time help him to maintain his Christian identity?" The question brings us face to face with a real challenge. Are these two concerns, however, necessarily mutually exclusive? When Christ is invited into our homes, He will einter in,

> *And he shall sit as a refiner and purifier of silver: and he shall purify the sons of Levi, and purge them as gold and silver, that they may offer unto the Lord an offering in righteousness* (Malachi 3:3).

You will notice that unless he is surrounded by examples, very little Christlike masculinity in your son will develop until he first sees Christ in you. Therefore, give him Jesus. Portray Christ before him. Give him guts, yes. Give him a sense of self-respect and dignity, yes. Psychology will concur that Peter Pan had guts (and nerve), and self-respect, but he never "grew up." Growing up and earning self-respect and dignity will not ripen into "...a pattern of good works: in doctrine shewing uncorruptness, gravity, sincerity, sound speech, that cannot be condemned" until a foundation be laid (see Tit. 2:7-8a). Seeing that, give your son Jesus "and when he is old, he will not depart from it" (Prov. 22:6b).

While the years draw nigh, may the roles and molds we adopt be unconditionally based on the Word of Truth. "Making a man out of the boy" is a *man-made* practice of molding, and it is exercised in contradiction to Scripture. "Toughening up" our sons and silently expecting them to take on our example of frigid insensitivity toward open contact is a trickle-down tradition that can be and *must be* broken. Picking up the tradition is habit-forming because first, it aids us in shying away from bonding with our sons, and secondly, because we are afraid to say the things to them that we *want to* but can't. We want to express our concern for them through those reassuring words that will sow into them a fulfilling sense of equilibrium—that is, a solid, level-headed, upstanding personal quality. We just can't get the words out. Hear this repeated, helpless heartbeat: "I *want to* but I *can't*" Who made us this way? For those of you fathers who *can* and *have* put these roles into practice, we need you to step forward and help spread the word. Its' getting late in our sons' and daughters' lives.

Each of us have watched and experienced how a mother will run to her eight-year-old Little League batter who while playing ball in the backyard runs, trips, and scrapes his knee. She'll lovingly pick him up, kiss his bruise, and hold him until he stops crying. Dad can do so much more. He can jump in and add something to this experience that will live in his spirit long after he outgrows Little League: "Don't be afraid of getting bruised. Did you kn ow that falling down and getting bruised is sometimes a sign of how much God loves young soldiers like you? And that watching your sores heal is actually like watching God Work? So let it all out, Sonny Boy, and we'll try it again when it stops hurting. In the meantime, you can ptich to me, instead." This can be hearty instruction for any kid who must eventually get a mental hold on the deeper meaning behind falling down, getting up, and going on. The played-out "boys don't cry" line is a boy's first nightmare lesson in learning how to hold things inside until he stubbornly understands pain as not only something that is not to be given a harmless outlet to be healed, but is a sign of weakness that will only " blow his cover." In plenty of cases, the only outlet a young man can find for his pain is through inflicting pain upon others, and that, Dad, is where fathering is immediately pointed at with a finger of accountability. It is vain conditioning that will confusingly shape these boys' perspectives when they arrive at the point in life when their significant "boy meets girl" relationships will call for responsible reactions to heavier dilemmas. Our boys don't really want to be "tough." Anybody can pick a fight, but only a man empowered by the exmaple of Christ can withstand the stormy weather associated with the seasons of manhood. In Christ, the effective rearing of our offspring involves pouring into them secure, confident, godly traits. For his own good, you might consider instilling in your son a sense of masculinity by helping him to be direct, decisive, and honest—yet firm. Won't you agree that these are the qualities of a strong, true, Christlike man?

We see Christ, while spending quaility time in fellowship with His disciples openly receiving John's love for Him, who "now there was learning upon Jesus' bosom..." (Jn. 13:24). Only a man who is totally confident of who he is could leave enough room in his heart for another man to cling to him with that kind of brotherly affection. Let us likewise give our boys the example of Jesus. We can't go wrong if we do.

Somehow, another chronic weakness in man's ability to cultivate and pass on self-truth has gone unaddressed and has left him hiding behind a facade. It is the facade of social affluence. How much quality time would you suppose is wasted rehearsing what we will tell our neighbors and church family when they approach you saying, "Praise the Lord Brother Jacob. So, how's your boy Joseph doing? I haven't seen him around lately." You answer, "Oh, me and Leah are so proud of him. He won a full scholarship to the university, he's already on the Dean's list, he's most definitely going to be a doctor, and his brothers were so happy for him that they got together and raised $2,560 to send him away in style." Now, Jacob, perhaps it is not everyone's business that Joseph was sold into Egypt by his brothers for $2,560, but the point is: the boy is seventeen years old. Just say, "He's away" and leave it at that. Who are you trying to impress? Although you wish these things for him, the fact that you would fabricate his whereabouts suggests that you desire his success for the wrong reasons.

What is the principle good in our motivation to work untiringly so that our children can complete their college educations and excel in the fields of medicine, law, and business, if we do not concurrently pray that they might be used of God in their area of expertise to treat illness, uphold the law, and restore the economy?

In all honesty, could it be that we do it simply to ensure that we will not feel left out of success-measuring conversations at family reunions, dinner parties, and at co-worker coffee clatches? Whether or not we are ready to admit to a common motive of our self-sacrifices, public opinion validates our ego by luring us away from our commitment to bring up our children in the nurture and admonition of the Lord (Eph. 6:4). Public opinion really matters to us! Why? To no surprise, children void of proper personality reinforcement and self-assurance grow up clinging to people who they believe have "arrived." Teenagers, especially, are easily impressed by the materialistic possessions, confident attitude, and ability of others to hide what may often be the same hurt that they endure, when in fact, these others just perhaps *conceal* it better. So, we find ourselves saying whatever we think will impress them, even if it means resorting to flattery, just so we will be accepted. This is all learned behavior. Who made us this way?

Outside of the home, the pursuit of good impressions and public acceptance are gradually becoming a preoccupation within the Church. For example, as good a thought as it may be to encourage our children to be well-seated in the church, Kingdom work must go on. It is undoubtedly a wonderful notion to desire our children to become pastors, deacons, missionaries to Africa, ministry leaders, etc., but it is not the Father's assignment to us for us to allow our parenting to take on ambitions of its own. In all fairness, imagine this: If only there were more "men" consulting the power of the cross and bringing back to their corporate administration "Light of the World" and "Salt of the Earth" standards for conducting business established upon the wisdom from above (see Jas. 3:17), the greater society could see God—but they're not. If there were men regularly gaining instructional insight through a consistent study of the Word as to what is godly and true (and what is not), they would bring holy principles back to government seats, pass godly laws, and for heaven's sake—save our nation! But they are not.

Meanwhile, the heavenly Father shakes His head in pity for us. He wants us to take note of how Christ walked among men and for us to develop His character in our children. In the end, nothing else matters. It is He Who projects the true image of His own Son upon man.

He created man in His own image (Gen. 1:26) and part of the image of God in man is found in this: We share His Fatherhood. God is the Father and all earthly parenthood is derived from Him. As He deals with us, thusly as His earthly children, according to this same threefold pattern, the message becomes evident: Fatherhood is to be shared.

One of the ways true fatherhood is shared is by enhancing our children's dependency upon Christ. Conducting "Hours of Prayer," allowing our sons to hear us talk with the Lord in the home, brings our relationship with Christ into reach of our children. When was the last time your children heard you pray? Real men "ought to always pray, and not...faint." (Luke 18:1b). It is neither a novelty to psychology nor an eye-opener to common sense that children are usually carbon copies of their parents. (My mom and my old man couldn't stand to hear me say that! I wonder why.) Fathers who pray, sire children who pray. Fathers who do not reach out, sire children who do not reach out, and the hurt that builds up from generation to generation only serves to become a family curse. And be sure, family curses are strong. Family curses are especially pivotal within in-law relationships. If a young man who has been perplexed by inherited tension marries into a family that has also been cursed, who is expected to get along with whom? This really hit home a few months ago when I saw an oversized U-haul truck moving my mother-in-law into our house. (It was just a bad dream.)

Still, in the course of what has been considered an inevitable feud, fathers can make an enormous statement without saying a word. Fathers, you can avoid years of conflict with your son-in-law if, for example, your daughter's judge of character has your perfect gentlemanly attention as its model. The daughter who receives this same gentlemanly attention from her father is being decorated with the stamp of self-identification that will blossom into a beautifully unreserved young lady who will make it known just where she expects the standards for conduct for her boyfriend or fiancé to begin. Our girls don't need Miss America pageantry and modern talk-show glamour panels in order to become successful, respectable women in relationships. They need fathers who will serve as the trend-setters. The only trend they will not likely accept is your suggestion of them to resign from their volunteer service (the one that makes your living room and your telephone grand central station for their classmates and, on weekends, the whole neighborhood). Take it from me, there's no hope.

By the same practice, the son who sees his father open the car door for his mother, pull out her chair when dining out, and buy her flowers "just because" will adopt that standard for conduct when he begins to date. On the other hand, if the son blatantly insists on marrying the devil's daughter, the warning should be given that he is sure to expect plenty of trouble from his father-in-law.

Acting out the role of "perfect gentleman" to your daughter, attentively loving your son, praying in the home, walking as Christ walked, and speaking words that bring a bond of peace between you and your wife, just as Christ spoke to those women who he encountered, makes the worthwhile parenting picture.

Does this sound like it's unreasonable or too much? Only to the *boy* it does. To the man who will please God in his manhood, it is the embodiment of the truths that will bring him there. Be proud of the universal influence God has given man. We, as fathers, possess the natural and spiritual power to launch greatness.

Where coaches, teachers, even pastors are unsuccessful, the God-fearing father can make the difference in a child's life. Take pride in the title "Father" as it bears synonymous meaning with *model* in word, deed, even in common courtesy. Think for a moment of the priceless smile on the face of that son who is helping his Dad work on the car. "Hand me the wrench," says Dad with his head tucked under the car, face-to-face with the muffler. The son reaches into the tool box, hands Dad the wrench, and Dad says, "Okay." Wrong answer, Dad. Stick your head out, make eye contact with your son, and tell him, "Thank you." The male parent who feels it is not necessary (or manly) to say, "Thank you," "Please," or "You're welcome" will find it that much more difficult to tell his son "I love you" when he needs to hear it most.

The seriousness of the psychological and emotional ramifications that can result from this kind of distant, mechanical, and alienated communication doesn't go away. It was stated in Chapter One that feelings of disappointment and rejection are often stored in the subconscious. Those of us who identify with this dilemma might find ourselves, tonight, having flashbacks of specific scenes from our childhood. In these scenes we saw our friends being lovingly embraced by their parents, and we wondered to ourselves, "Why don't my parents touch me like that?"

What is it, exactly, that keeps us from reaching out and touching our children when they're hurting? We don't know how. More than ever, Jesus is calling, today. He's saying, "I will show you." He brings us to the cross where He Himself was wounded. Touch His hands, brothers. The pain in your heart will be healed by the wounds of His hands. His manly power will release you from those strongholds and replenish your empty vessel with the fullness that you have searched for. Our inner man weeps with turmoil pleading, "There's something on the inside that longs to be a man, but how can I be a father, when I've never been a son!"

The first step to take in this absolutely critical process of molding and shaping points directly back to the constancy of prayer. When hurting sons hear their hurting fathers pray, they will pray, and the prayer-answering God Who calms all our unspoken fears will make intercession on each behalf. More than that, He will bring each of you in the Spirit back to each other (see Mal. 4:6). By faith, when the Spirit at last brings you face-to-face with your estranged son, take advantage of the moment and dare to be the father you long to be by bringing your son's hand (which should fit perfectly into the mold and shape of your own) into yours. When he looks at you with eyes that ask the question "Why are you holding my hand?" tell him, "Because it feels good to be bonded to you, to nurture you, and to allow destiny to flow through our unbreakable link." While you're holding his hand, pray him through his fears and insecurities. Encourage him, walk with him through embarrassment, stand with him in times of disappointment, reach over and lift his head up, and say to him "You can make it." Say it over and again, "If I make it, I'm going to see to it that you make it!" Your son will see a genuine hero in you, and your relationship with him will never be the same.

If along the way, Dad, you begin to feel as though your relationship between you and your son is not "normal," lift up your head, open your mouth and shout, "Praise God!" because according to my barometer, the "normal" has not been working.

The Sainted
Sister's Passion

Chapter Three

What's Wrong
With My Jacob?

"What's wrong with my Jacob?" Mothers and wives want to know. Needless to say, mothers are the first woman a boy naturally loves as his source of physical nourishment. Denial of this dependence will follow him into any and every subsequent male-female relationship and allow for complicated puberty, adolescent, and adulthood relationships. Classroom methodologies that misunderstand boys, social structures that label them, and parental guidelines that either confuse or neglect them cause their complications to become that much more startling. The typical combination of these situations can take a traumatic toll on the boy's ability to breed healthy emotions, and so, he doesn't. By personal observation, I have found it safe to suggest that because women are keenly more receptive to sharing and exchanging honest feelings, men perhaps become that much more reluctant to "open up" to their male constituents for fear that their openness will be labeled as "womanlike."

To gain victory over such a common fear is to gain victory over other pertinent barriers that incur within male-female relationships. All things considered, we still hide, run, and put up defenses to avoid our wives' question when our behavior becomes complicated, stubborn, and silent. They ask, as lovingly and sincerely as they know how, "What's wrong?" Later, their tone will shift from a tender plea to demanding fighting words, "Why don't you tell me what's wrong?" Women in marriages that have lasted for 20, 30, and 40 years who have asked this question more than likely know the problem. Their reverence for God and honor for their husbands keeps them from pursuing it further. And women, although you often shed tears on your husband's behalf, such a demonstration of humility and exercise of wisdom is certain to bring to you manifold rewards in the end as a women whose price in the sight of God is far above rubies. (See Proverbs 31:10.) God bless you.

The wife who faithfully honors her husband as the Scriptures advise will honor the most prevalent truths about his struggles through the six progressive stages of manhood, his struggles to please her, and his struggle to be a conscientious, loving spouse. And the truth is: Most of the time, the struggling husband, regardless of the stage he is in, is simply doing the best that he can to fight his way through the tests and move on. Perhaps this is not so by our standards, but the Scripture's instructions to the Christian family is to not submit to other standards in the first place, nor be influenced by the status quo. Standards are born of society, but understanding is born of sure commitment and wisdom. I trust that after seeking this understanding of man, that a new birth takes place in you, seasoning you daily with the priceless attributes of a saintly woman of wisdom.

To offer a small element of encouragement, if any of these things characterize your "Jacob's" outlet, consider this: Pornographic indulgences, wife-battering, and infliction of mental anguish are not so much about stress and job-related frustrations as it is about male insecurity, inadequacy, and feelings of helplessness. That's just it. We compensate one hundred different ways for one generalized problem—fear. The class of fear varies widely among them at progressive stages of their manhood. Some men fear become "womanlike" through letting go of their anxiety. Others fear the opinion of the "fellas" with fear and trembling; and when it comes to the acceptance of their manliness, what the "fellas" think matters almost as much as (if not more than) the symbolism of his wedding band. A great deal more men fear the release of built-up emotions. Carrying around strong, childhood troubles, and disappointments is their conceptualized base of strength, sort of like lifting weights—no pain, no gain.

Many wives hope to gain some insight into their husbands' pain, and into their own as well. However, when hope seems distressingly non-existent, they may find themselves attempting to escape their husbands' suppressed distress by searching for answers in the pages of romance literature, and television. They may even look for answers in the classroom seats of community colleges that offer courses in women's studies. The quest for knowledge demonstrates true commitment on the part of a wife, mother, or daughter. I have watched this from varying angles and have observed that they leave these classes still asking the same questions of their husbands, from the same point of view, because no one ever suggested to them that conversely, the Sainted Sister's enrollment should be in classes that deal with men's issues. Such a study would probably offer far greater insight. However, to my knowledge, no such classes exist—anywhere.

It is significant to further observe, that with a notable lack of interest in self-study, we as men do not begin to deal with crises in manhood or the questions of our wives until her bags are packed and she is leaving us to deal with our own backlashes of denial. It is then that a reality check is done, and the man realizes, "Maybe there is a problem." Invariably, men in denial do not begin to conduct self-examinations until the crises find them in the contestation stages of divorce, or in the preliminary application phase of job hunting, again. It calls for a closer-to-home experience, and sometimes even a tragedy (God forbid) to awaken our quest for understanding.

In the meantime, woman of God, continue to be faithful in your search for the deeper understanding of the woman who God has created in you, and continue the role you desire to fulfill in unconditionally loving the man God has created in your husband. This is strictly a woman of God/voice of God relationship. Leave the tabloids to those whose misunderstanding and misdirection have driven them to the point where they have apparently given up on (or never entered into) the listening room of prayer; it is in that room where we will hear answers through humbly seeking His face. That's a promise. (See 2 Chronicles 7:14.) Praying on your husbands' behalf and initiating open communication is in proper focus only when you know what stage of his manhood you are praying him through, and the types of conversations that will bring out the positive features of that stage.

With every detail of encouragement offered here to the wife as the concerned vessel, I believe it can be popularly agreed upon that through our marriage experience, singles friendships, and attention to mother-child influence that women are remarkably sensitive to things to which men pay very little attention. I can recall a few months after my daughter was born, I heard what sounded to me to be an irritating cry coming from the adjacent nursery. It was rather strange to me that my wife, who could not possibly have been asleep, did not go see what was wrong. I remember tiresomely mumbling, "Honey, the baby's crying." She calmly said, "Nothing's wrong." I snapped back, "How do you know? Can't you hear her crying?" Again, still nonchalant, she said, "Nothing's wrong. She's just hungry." Her confident tone let me know that as a woman, and especially a mother, that she was a great deal more sensitive than myself, as a man, and father. The same holds true in their discernment of our inhibitions and avoidance behavior as husbands. Male sensitivity is not nearly as instinctive as female sensitivity. The sensitive male usually acquires his sensitivity from his mother, or from a wholesome learning relationship with his wife. Sadly, this is almost never learned from his father. What *is* it that impairs man's expressed sense of brotherly caring, fatherly sensitivity, and conjugal openness?

"What's wrong with my Jacob? How did his mother deal with this? Or did she?" The Bible records that Rebekah, mother of Jacob (and his twin, Esau) a first time mother herself perceived.

> ...*the children struggled together within her; and she said, if it be so, why am I thus? And she went to inquire of the Lord. And the Lord said unto her, Two nations are in thy womb, and two manner of people shall be separated from thy bowels; and the one people shall be stronger than the other people; and the elder shall serve the younger* (Genesis 25:22-23).

The woman of wisdom may never understand *why* but she will understand *what*. She should also be heedful that her husband's inability to respond sensitively to his own needs, much less the needs of others should be the passionate subject of her prayer life.

During a recent counseling session, one of the sisters from the local assembly whose marriage was in despair shared with me a rather awakening dream that came as an answer to her many months of prayer. Although confused over the emotional barricade that her husband had built in the middle of their relationship, "Beverly," this young devoted wife, vividly recalled the scene of a baby boy lying in bed beside her. The baby was crying. As she began to mother him, nurse him, and care for him, she found herself shaken out of her sleep altogether distraught, pleading, "My Lord! Is this the answer to me and 'Bill's' problems? Is this what it will take for me to save my marriage? Having a baby? Oh, please, no." The Spirit of the Lord quickly fixed her understanding and replied, "My daughter, this helpless child whom I have shown you is not one that you will bring forth, but it is the very one to whom you are espoused. The baby boy who lies beside you is your husband." The voice of the Spirit exhorted her to sympathize with the fact that "Bill" was trapped in a stage from which he could not be released except he first receive the nurturing, care, and attention that he apparently whined for through his childhood, and miserably, in his marriage.

The challenge set before "Beverly", as a sainted wife, is to tender such treatment with a silent understanding of her husband's boyhood cries with an equal understanding that such attention will help him progress onward to a loftier stage in his manhood. Sadly, intimacy in marriage relationships scares many people because they were never intimately connected with their parents. The true issue of intimacy in marriage means placing an emotional covenant and commitment all the way around your spouse in their hurt, until your perfect love casts out their fear.

This may not happen by your next wedding anniversary, but if you promise not to become impatient and unyoke yourself from the good things—the things he does better than anyone else, the things he says that make you laugh, as well as the things he *doesn't say* that would make you cry—you, my sister, will have prepared for the Lord a holy table to come between the two of you and speak your passion to your "Jacob" in words that he can understand. As you keep this emotional covenant tightly embraced around him, you will see that it is the only way that he will hear your speechless emotions groaning, "I want to feel your pain, or at least release you of it. I want to be so knitted with you that whatever is wrong, you will allow me to draw it out."

In the meantime, however, the woman of wisdom must also remain subject to consistent and non-hypocritical demands of her husband. If you want your "Jacob" to spill-out his insecurities and emotional struggles, you must not become offended when he lets go of things that run far deeper than your hard-earned suspicions had anticipated. Along with that, if your husband's expression of his fears causes you to become uncomfortable and to act out disapproval, you can be assured that your discomfort will clam him up for life. The next time that he begins to express himself following your expression of disapproval, it will not be a release of his insecurities but a blast of his primary male feeling—anger brought on by a compounded sense of mistrust. Pray, my sisters, to be sure that you are prepared for his openness. Some of the things he will say may startle you so brace yourself, listen carefully and try not to provoke his transparency beyond his willingness to go into details. It could mean more trouble. Take it from a man, there's a Ralph Kramden in us all, and after "The Honeymoon" he's depending on you, "Alice" to be sensitive enough not to bring up anything that has been declared "closed for discussion." In other words, if you've never been to the moon, don't give him any ideas.

Therefore, in your prayers again, for the protection of the royalty and honor in your marriage, remember: He's probably doing the best he can with the hurt that he didn't ask for in the first place, or (more historically speaking) "in the beginning." At the beginning of the lawful marital relationship, scripturally inspired vows were exchanged that were meant to convey a commitment in the face of God and to assign husband-wife roles according to His holy ordinance. God's holy ordinance convicts, but commitment must come from man. Your "Jacob" who could not count on his father to be there for him, cannot trust anyone today with his feelings—not even himself.

In the case of believing wives with unbelieving husbands, wives in this kind of marriage ought not pray necessarily for their husbands' salvation. Sooner or later the believing wife will sanctify the unbelieving husband. (See 1 Corinthians 7:14.) Pray first, that you might not dangerously provoke his insecurities, and pray secondly, that you might be daily inspired to live out a godly life so that when God saves your "Jacob" (and He will), that upon his acceptance of Christ, he might not resist the wrestling of the Father to deliver him completely. It is through this system of dealing with the source of his complex conduct for the sake of spiritual growth that holiness becomes progressive. (And again, whether or not psychological scholarship is ready to support theological principles, before this analysis is concluded we are going to find ourselves at the beckon of God's requirement for holiness!)

At any cost, let the natural, although sometimes crippled, developmental process now begin. Full-fledged, godly manhood, like all great things, takes time to achieve, and it must advance through its six general prescribed stages. We must not interrupt that process, but we must take the time to understand it for what it is. For example, verbal dissatisfaction with your husband for being "just a man" in the hope that he would become a "just man" is a value and character judgment, which no family member is qualified to make. It leaves the natural properties of his current phase of manhood out of the picture. God called his creation "Adam," which is to say that he was His masterpiece in the form of man, made from the dust. His very being was compacted with character, qualities, and unique abilities innocently self-contained to make a distinct mark upon the earth.

Whoever planted and watered this seed could either have been a great, conscientious harvester, or a negligent, misinformed stranger to the soul of this man. If the latter be the case, your "Jacob" could very well have been suspended in his *Adam* (Stage 1) phase of manhood.

In this event, put to work your measure of faith, the power of prayer, the spirit of agreement and walk him through it (see Amos 3:3). He doesn't necessarily have to hear you bellowing out across the daily activities of the household. Keep the conversation between the two of you— you and the Holy Ghost. It might not be a bad idea to crank up your prayer by requesting that you be led away from the common temptation of dragging third parties into the picture. Leave third parties out of your marriage, and tell God alone about it. Third parties are prone to interject their opinionated questions to women, such as "Why do you remain in a marriage where there is giving and communicating of needs from your side only? Must every opportunity to share quality time with each other boil down to a strain, unless it begin and end with the pleasures of sexual relations?" This complaint of women brings nothing new at all to our study.

Nevertheless, in answer to the question, "Why do women remain in marriages that seem to be nothing more than a physical relationship?" The answer is, that even though you sainted sisters take rightful pleasure in the sexual relationship with your husbands, you have remained ever fastened to the hope that you both will one day accentuate each other's weaknesses, especially those which cause conjugal tension and offer you both something *more* to look forward to. From that compromise, your desire to build a well-rounded marriage becomes apparent.

The differences in attitude among couples on this subject are as uniquely contrasting in reasoning as is their independent learning strategies. Since research and observations have indicated that men and women learn differently, none of these things should move you past logically concluding that their understanding of roles in marriage, and their expectations and perspectives in relationships— especially as it relates to sharing emotions—are equally as different. That is to say that because men and women learn differently, they adapt differently. Keep in mind, if a man has not been adequately supervised by his dad or been subject to an example of how to express himself in ways outside of sexual atmosphere; if he has not been taught how to make his wife feel special, wanted, appreciated, and respected on a day-to-day basis with attentive gestures and inclinations of the heart; he will let go of passions the only way he knows how—with his body.

Throughout your husband's walk through the next five stages of manhood, remember that each corresponds to a progressive level of development. First the typical *Zakar* (phallic), personality (Stage 2) is in fact restricted to sexual relations requiring no verbal expression. It does not pause for a call in the middle of the day just to say, "I love you." The *Zakar* is not prone to stop on his way home from work and pick up a bouquet of flowers for you. It is highly unlikely that he will arrive at home and seeing that you have had an exhausting day, act upon the considerate motive to run your bath water, order you to relax and finally go to bed while he takes the kids out to dinner and for some fun activities for an hour or two. If he hasn't arrived there yet, my sister, let it grow.

When you may be asking him to be different and when you're comparing him with other men in conversations with your girlfriends (a reproachable "no-no"), try to catch yourself, hang up the phone in the name of Jesus and immediately supplicate on his behalf, straight through that stage. Again if that means it's *that* important to you, tell God about it. Be ever mindful of how comparisons to others insult your husband's individuality. "Why can't he be a warrior, a doer, a conqueror like his brother Esau?" Because he had an unfair start in life.

After all, your husband was the one that was destined to come out first, but Esau pushed him aside. Remember your father-in-law Isaac spent quality time with Esau and never with Jacob. When you look into your Jacob's eyes, can't you see the mistreatment he has endured all his life? Can't you see him being made the spectacle of ridicule at family gatherings? Can't you see him cringing to himself while being laughed at because of his harmlessly smooth features. Can't you see his brother Esau running and playing with the other boys and leaving Jacob behind? Can't you hear the indictments they assigned to his intellect, his imagination, his sexuality, and his love for God? He knew he was a real man deep down inside; but every time he opened his mouth to defend himself, Esau would punch him, and their father, Isaac, would take up for Esau! Can't you see, woman of God, where your Jacob got stuck in life. I'm sure you can understand for the first time why he went through life hurting women simply to prove that he was a man.

Is it any wonder that his ego seems to come ahead of every household matter. Can you now more clearly understand why he is motivated by competitiveness and why his dinner table conversations sparkle with sports stories. He makes his own "to do" in *whatever he can do,* and he's not satisfied until *he does.* If that's the story of his behavior, as boring and pointless as it may be strike you, he must prove himself. Even if it means being the subject of failure after failure, a man must prove his "warriorship." At this stage (Stage 3), his spirit cries to become a conquering hero, a champion, *Gibbor.* Sshhh, what he doesn't know is that you and God have been having extensive discussions about this, and as far as you and God are concerned, he's already "more than a conqueror" (see Rom. 8:37). So, there's nothing really wrong with this stage, ladies. Chances are, it may only last temporarily before moving on to the next stage. But whether long-term or short-term, be extra careful not to lose sight of the insulting, demeaning consequences of having a brother Esau, who was charged with his parent's pride by the very meaning of the name they gave him—"to accomplish, to advance, to fulfill, and to finish"—and was pampered with parental encouragement. Your "Jacob" was not. Should you find yourself slowly grasping hold of this reality that haunts the hearts of men, you'll be prepared to sacrifice your own interests for the sake of his. Regardless of how interesting least night's PTA meeting was, you might have to keep the highlights of it to yourself (at least until he gets to Stage 5). You're not fooling yourself if you ignore the fact that your evening time together can become even more frustrating if you're in the mood for romance and he's got his eyes on the remote control in between his salad and soup. You're a woman who knows that the dinner table is the perfect place to begin tossing around your charm. But depending on what kind of day he had at the job, the gym, or the deacon's meeting, if you sense that he's likely to cut off your hints for sentimental bliss and candlelight conversations with his "conquering hero" doozies that open up with the story about the "one that got away" and end up with the time he stood nose-to-nose with a polar bear or the time he single-handedly rescued his platoon from the enemy's secret attack, you'll know that each time you sit down to dine you can take this simple precaution while he's blessing the food: Touch and agree with him, and silently pray him through. You can do this with specific concentration and focus becaue you now know that what your Jacob needs is to feel successful. Therefore he needs to tell himself he is in the presence of those to whom he already feels naturally superior.

Ask the Father for a touch that will bring you in touch with his wounds of having been rejected and born with a predisposition to becoming a "deceiver." His healed scars will one day serve as the needed strength to keep the family together. Until then, you will find that among other things, this stage will be typified by numb reactions to disappointment, withdrawal, and sometimes apprehensions to trusting others—even you.

Wounds are an inevitable, though probably most helpful consequence for surviving what I call the "co-op stages"—the cause for one (Wounded, *Enosh*, Stage 5) works along with the results of the previous passage into the other (Warrior, *Gibbor*, Stage 4). For instance, some "Jacobs" go through life hurting, and in turn, hurting others. On the other hand, others remain at the Wounded Stage long enough to help another Jacob deal with his or her hurt. He is advancing from the best angle of this stage that will land him safely at a place in manly sensitivity where he will be able to heal the wounds of others. You can help him to feel good about both these stages by lifting his confidence with positive feelings of being a "Warrior." Make it a point to mention of his willingness to go out into the jungle of life everyday, to kill anything that might interfere with him feeding, clothing, and providing for his family. You can encourage him in his "Wounded" stage by mentioning how special it is that this same man would be willing to take the bullet, lay down his life for his family. This is *your* man, your Jacob. By this time you might find yourself surprised by the fact that there are far more issues on board than you thought. But when you stand back and take a distant view of his journey from off-shore, you'll see that as he passes from one stage to another, the smoother he sails.

As he walks more confidently, and into the "Warrior" stage, it may seem that his self-assurance is moving in reverse order to Stage 3 ("Wounded Male"). Don't worry, he's not going backwards. A man whose wounds are in the mending process is too emotionally drained to respond in any fashion other than compassionately to the pain of those whom he loves. A man who has humbled himself after being healed of hurt will bring quicker relief to his marriage, children, and church than a "warring" man. Physical and industrial strength doesn't always equal spiritual sophistication. You, my sister, are now in the perfect position to assume an enormously critical role in his passage through the "Wounded," *Enosh* stage into the "Mature, Reborn Ruler" (*Ish*, Stage 5) stage.

Careful though, the tongue that prays for "higher ground," and a loftier stage in manhood in God for her husband, must not proceed with *cursing* out of the same lips: "You know I hate it when you block the driveway the way you do! It makes me sick!" My sister, whatsoever things are said in the right tone, if there be any virtue, if there be any praise, think on these things. What would it profit you as a wife to gain the attention and regard of your husband who is bordering on the Mature Male (*Ish*) stage, and lose your influence by irrationally putting him on the defensive side over trivial matters?

Observe in Second Samuel 6:14, when David brought the ark up into Jerusalem out of the house of Obededom, he danced before the Lord and worshipped Him in the Spirit. Michal (who should have either remained silent, or have danced with him) only interfered with God's blessing for her husband, *and herself* by criticizing and "picking" at him.

Ladies, be careful at this stage *how* you offer criticism. As petty as it sounds, a man can be internally wounded again at this point, and in some instances, may not be able to fully recover without the help of the heavenly Father. However, it should be noted for observation, that if you cannot celebrate with your husband the recovery of the ark, perhaps you have your own set of unresolved conflicts to be addressed, and peradventure he is not the sole problem. Instead, you might elect this approach: "Honey, you know, Dear, sometimes when you block the driveway, I have to park down the street, and the dark walk up the street to the house makes me frightened. Actually, Honey," while stroking him and savoring his attention, "sometimes I don't have to walk back to the house because the neighbor's dog chases me, and I wind up running to the house." You woman of God, have been born with influence! Now is the time to discernably put it to work.

What kind of man, whether a struggling *boy* in a man's body, or a seasoned sage in the bounty of his manhood would negatively respond to such a tender and honest (and rather arousing) request? Returning home each day to that kind of attention will relieve tension, build mutual respect, and will grant your Jacob the essential space for God to work on him and *in him*. You will play a pivotal role in endorsing his candidacy for the next and final stage—the "Sage" (*Zaken*, Stage 6) because of God's favor for *you*.

It is the "Sage" who makes his spiritual investments with his hard-earned daily bread in those things that will reap good spiritual fruit for himself and his family. His God is his guide. His anointing is his appetite. Yes, the mature male will take the hands of his sons and lead them out of the counsel of the ungodly mentioned in Psalms 1:1 and into the pastures of spiritual prosperity and devout reverence. When his children are old, they will bring forth the fruit of the seed God gave him to plant in them.

Ultimately, when he himself is old, in his daily meditations and worship to God for having survived and successfully passed from the *Adam* Stage to the *Zaken* Stage, and for finally reaching the ripe stage in life of "Sage" his wisdom will no doubt cause him to realize that he may not have made it past the "Wounded" stage had it not been for you seeking the Lord on his behalf. His meditations will remain fixed upon the law of the Lord, day and night. To his spouse, his brethren, his seed, and their seed, he shall sit among them as a source of wisdom, a strong and stable tree planted by the rivers of water (See Psalm 1:3.)

Woman of God, if you find yourself battling with confusing answers in your venture to clearly see "what's wrong" with your Jacob, ask God to get it out of him. Ask the Father to meet your "Jacob" man-to-man to get to the root of the problem. After all, God was listening when you made your vows, and He's listening to your spoken requests for the understanding that will help you to keep them and to heal your "Jacob."

God is not unrighteous that He would forget your self-sacrifices of love for your husband—yes, for better or for worse. As for your "Jacob" things are already becoming "better" within him because he has you beside him. And you must obviously care a great deal for him. Otherwise you would not have taken this time to try and understand what is wrong, what went wrong, and what can be made right. Your prayers, understanding, patience, love, and commitment to him until death are sure to bring out the very best in you both. You have patiently sought the Kingdom of God. May the heavenly Father, as promised, award you the desires of your heart. (See Matthew 6:33.)

Different and Indifferent Strokes

Chapter Four

Steal Away to Dad

Does this sound familiar? Your 11-month-old son took his first step alone, but you missed it because you were at work. Or, he walked alone for the first time in the family room, but you were in the den at the time. No big deal, your wife will recreate all the excitement for you when she tells you about it. There will come a season, about 12 years later, when a boy takes his first step towards manhood. When he does, Mom won't be able to tell you about it because Junior's first step toward manhood will be his first step taken away from her maternal grip. As a pastor and father, my spirit earnestly groans to see the hearts of fathers and sons merged, especially at this point in a young man's development. If situations have arisen that have severed the relationship, my faith rests upon the hope that this discourse will move away the hurt and will call for their reconciliation before Dad's emotional distance causes him to lose sight of this truth: Being a man, in times like these means being under pressure. And being a young man (or the son of a young man) means being under double pressure.

Routinely, any man whose absent or unavailable father has left him empty from this need, the same man will put forth little or no effort toward bonding when he has his own children. This will become especially obvious when the responsibility is laid upon him to assume the privilege of calling out his son into manhood. There is no dispute; when a boy reaches puberty, filled with the powerful physical stirring of his emerging manhood, the father's role becomes critical. If at this point, the boy is not called out and away from his mother by his father, his years of love invested in her will remain unavailable to the women he might love later in life. This rite of passage from the abiding care of his mother into the ranks of men must be made available with delicate authority.

Sons whose fathers were not called out from their mothers at the appropriate stage in life are at a definite risk. In the father's untold resentment he misemploys the necessary bonding with his son under the popular cop-out "deal with it." Conversely, sons who take the initiative to reach out to their fathers are taking the risk of being rejected by the remark, "If I survived without attention, affection, and nurturing, so can you." Still many will uphold that being a "real man" means being able to ignore the need, and journey onward without it being met. Believe it or not, the Father *does* understand.

Careful though, this transitional bonding must not proceed through willful disobedience of the son toward his mother or by alluding to conduct that compares one parent with the other and, as a result, creates an in-house custody battle. If every mother viewed her motherhood as an outgrowth of God's favor upon her as a chosen vessel in bringing into the world a chosen leader, servant, and future father, she would be less inclined to dominate his flourishing manhood. Well-intentioned mothers (by definition, there is no other kind) will qualify such royal preparation in their sons' lives by stepping back and allowing the Father God to bring him up and out into His predestined will. An earthly father's influential custody of his son is God's ideal resource for completing the work of manhood in him.

Nevertheless, maternal instinct has not revealed to mothers the emotional impact of detaching themselves from their own sons for their own sake. Certainly the bio-emotional bond between mother and son is a two-edged sword: It will either cut into the bond and allow the son to be placed into and feel comfortable in the company of men, securing a sense of belonging and identification with manliness; or it will slice the father's efforts in two, resist his privileges, and divide the boy's identification as a whole. As permanent in its basis as the mother-son relatioship is, the influence and sphere of discipline is only temporal. Therefore, fatherhood must be interwoven into the mother's efforts, even in the son's early age. He must also be prepared at the appointed time to continue with coaching, connecting with, and witnessing his son's natural metamorphosis into adulthood. From a biologically changing male's point of view, when all of the confusing changes of life leave him torn between the toys of boyhood and the responsibilities of manhood, what makes the real difference is when Dad is there to offer his experienced guidance.

Vividly, I can remember the air of the house as we played as children. But as I heard the call of my sister or brother, "Daddy's Home," things changed. He didn't have to make a grand entrance, neither did he make any public speeches; just his presence, knowing he was there, offered a security that was matchless. No bad guys would get us now, because "Daddy's Home." Daddy's presence was enough to bring an unchallenged zone of comfort, a comfort that could not be attained from any other source. We would have bet our whole allowance (25 cents), that he was 18 feet tall, had hands twice the size of a watermelon (honest), and that we could swing from his arm even when he was too tired to make a muscle from a hard day's work. We didn't know that we didn't have a lot, and at the same time, it was irrelevant because the whole neighborhood had the same. It was also irrelevant to us that he had dropped out of school in the third grade to help work and support the family. Seemingly, the only thing that mattered was the giant security blanket he felt he had to throw over the house, and the only reward for it all was "Daddy's Home." But six years later, my outlook on life—my Dad, Mom, girls, Lyndon B. Johnson, the NFL, Vietnam, and especially myself—was culturally (and psychologically) different. I was growing up, changing, and discovering who I was.

As pubescent boys discover their sexuality, whether they have a wholesome sense of their identity or not, the father's security blanket becomes increasingly important. If by chance the son in emotional transition becomes potential bait lured away by the one-track mindedness of having girl after girl, the father who is able to identify with these associated symptoms will surely treat his son with fatherly strokes of understanding. This exclusive relationship based on openness of communication will mark the private union of exchanged fears through which closely-knit father-son bonding will bring relief. Indeed, it must do more than bring seasonal relief, it must be familiarized by an already existing openness and contact. On the whole, the father who learns how to speak, listen, and share quality time with his son during his formative years, will be that much more successful in entering into the boy's life at a period when he starts to feel the circulating race of his hormones telling him that "there's another man in the house besides Dad." A prolonged entrance into his life just won't work. If the bonding is delayed, his peers will likely become his source of influence.

Not only has God *not* placed this "nurturing" (as discussed in Ephesians 6) into the authority of his peers, but common adult sense dictates that they cannot direct him with values based on useful life experience. Peers cannot steer him toward building commitments in responsible monogamous relationships. And by the time he begins to consider this kind of "serious" behavior, the last person whose advice will be solicited is Mom's. Who does that leave?

What all this means is that it is now time for Dad to step completely into the picture and help him to deal with the issues of life. Although it may at times require reading between the lines of a barely audible mumble in response to the question, "Where have you been?" or his springtime habit of mysteriously disappearing from the house between 5 p.m. and 8 p.m. dripping with your most expensive brand of cologne. Reading between these lines can get to be frustrating, but we as fathers cannot afford to miss any signals and fail to receive the message that our teen boys send to us. The catch is, he doesn't plan to tell you where he's going. He'll only tell you when things start to get scary and he doesn't know what to do next. You may think that his asking what to do when her gum gets stuck in his braces is absurd, but to a 15-year-old whose self-esteem could explode at any moment, it's a big deal. All of this is new to him, and it takes only an available Dad to make him feel comfortable in talking about it.

Teach him as best you can, Dad—man-to-man—first of all, how to respect women. Explain to him that his newly-discovered daydreaming figure is not to be exploited, but respected. Instruct him to respect and honor the beauty that woman brings to man's life. The earlier he understands this, the less susceptible he will be to instability in relationships. Naturally, because the girls in whom he will take an interest in cannot be viewed in his eyes with the same adoration and precious esteem as he views mother, a solid lesson in "people appreciation" from a father's point of view should mold his. In a word, fathers who call their sons out from their mothers' protectiveness and often single-handed parenting, must therefore be qualified to do so. Remember, by the way, that your son is "stealing away" to you to adopt a way of life that will assist him in living life to the fullest.

Prior to and subsequent to "stealing away," the societal and parental attitude, although admittedly a double standard, remains "boys will be boys." However, at the age of 35 when as a husband, father, leader, and teacher, who never bonded with his own father, "Junior" finds that he still knows only how to express himself through sex, the *boy*, sad to say, is still being *a boy*. That being the case, what is the son of "the boy" expected to become—a psychologically-adjusted champion of God-fearing prudence? On the brighter side, from time to time, out of bitterness and determination to break the curse (see the example of Joseph in Chapter Seven), evolves a real man dedicated to the role of a Spirit-led leader of the home, church, and society. The question is, are you ready for a new name? Are you prepared to live up to the name that is not compartmentalized by the shallow definition of manhood as it relates to the discovery of sexuality? If so, tonight is your night!

True enough, as irresistibly inviting as the act of sex may be, all of the pleasure of sex can never produce or replace the joy that a young man receives from knowing that he is a whole man who has been nurtured and groomed by his own father for the natural changes that come with adolescence. That knowledge will equip him with the strength to lead the nations. But if there is first no joy of the Lord, there is no strength (see Neh. 8:10).

Fathers, can you think of any other person who is more qualified to plant the truth into your son concerning the sacred value and strength of his ripening manhood? What he does not know could actually nullify your covenant with God and the unrevealed promise He has given to all of your descendants. No young man should enter or exit his pubescence without being called to sit at the feet of his father to discover the clout his sexual nature carries in the will of God for the future of mankind. The seed God has implanted into his loins must not be allowed to spill to the ground and become moistened with the dirt of the earth (Gen. 38:8). Not only does this displease God, but it places him at the hand of God's wrath to be cut off from his destiny. With the help of his mother, Jacob tricked Esau out of the blessing of the firstborn by disguising himself as Esau. The Jacobic history repeated itself when his grandson's wife (through

Judah) disguised herself as a harlot, not only to obtain the blessing of Judah's firstborn but to protect herself against Judah's possible proposition after she had been widowed. Whereas if Judah's son, Onan, had not been given to vile affection by sexually wasting his seed during intercourse, he would not have been slain, and might very well have become one of the forefathers of the Messiah! (See Matthew 1:1-3.) Fathers, we must teach our boys as soon as they begin to discover their sexuality not to waste their seed for any reason or for anyone!

Once the unforseen damage of a young man's premarital relations is inevitably uncovered, it will somehow agitate and haunt his future. And the struggles to repair such damage might cast great tension upon his marriage, covenant relationships, and ability to avail himself to his own sons as someone to "steal away" to.

Young men, take note that the passive logic your father may drift to in excusing himself from this critical period in your life, can (and more than likely will) engender in you feelings of resentment. If you have not had a personal experience at the cross of Jesus, you will find it difficult to understand that "God is near" when your body begins maturing to your own surprise and your emotions begin fluctuating like the swing of a pendulum. And if all the while no one seems to be listening and your opinion of your father is manifested by reactions of anger and resentment, pray for the discipline to put away [these] childish things" (see 1 Cor. 13:11). You're becoming a man now. When your teenage disgust comes out, the heavenly Father hears the disgust (which is actually hurt) in your tone toward your mother's intermittent discipline, when, in fact, your anger is not even about Mom. Actually, all you really want is for your father to walk by and just touch you every once in a while; because he doesn't, your maturing process becomes unfairly stunted by pain. Adolescent pain in any class of society is dangerously severe. Statistically, it results in manic-depressive behavioral disorders and often suicide. But you take it out on Mom. Before becoming angry with her, please try to understand that as a woman your mother cannot completely understand the kind of emotional shock you are experiencing.

Do you, young man (or father) feel like you have been denied certain privileges? From the bleachers of after school football games to the active attention-seeking behavior that abound, I hear your answer, *"Yes, I do. Help!"* Be that as it may, do not by any means replace your display of honor and respect with outrage and disrespect. The duty of the young man is to maintain his integrity by protecting his father's (Ex. 20:12; Prov. 10:1, 20:20: Tit. 2:6-10). Obedient or disobedient to the original commands of the Lord, the promise of longevity does not hang upon a contingency of having the "ideal" or "perfect" parents, but upon exercising unconditional honor toward them.

Jacob, who hurt for his father's endorsement and attention found himself alone in his hurt and bewildered after having been awakened out of sleep. He declared:

> *Surely the Lord is in this place; and I knew it not.*
> *And he was afraid, and said, How dreadful is this*
> *place! This is none other than the house of God, and*
> *this is the gate of heaven* (Genesis 28:16b-17).

Young men, the point is, that when the time comes for you to biologically and psychologically grow into manhood, if you are not inducted into the company of your earthly father, stand strong in your glorious strength with the faith that your heavenly Father is nearby (Prov. 20:29).

Therefore, as you wait for your father's attention, don't let it be said of you that you were talking back to Dad in

God's presence and you didn't even know it. Don't let it be said of you that you were cursing Dad's coldness in God's holy presence and you didn't even know it—don't let it be said! Let it be said that you waited on your father to call you out unto manhood—he didn't—and so you waited on the Lord and He renewed your strength (see Is. 40:31). God sees and He knows. Moreover, the heavenly Father has a way of replenishing our earthly emptiness.

Listen to His words to you:

Why sayest thou, O Jacob, and speakest, O Israel, My way is hid from the Lord...? Hast thou not known? hast thou not heard, that the everlasting God, the Lord, the Creator of the ends of the earth, fainteth not, neither is weary? There is no searching of His understanding. He giveth power to the faint; and to them that have no might He increaseth strength. Even the youths shall faint and be weary, and the young men shall utterly fall: But they that wait upon the Lord shall renew their strength; and they shall mount up with wings as eagles; they shall run and not be weary; they shall walk, and not faint (Isaiah 40:27-31).

I have one final point. Calling out our sons from their mothers' single-handed parenting is not always the consequence of simply the possible emotional absence of Dad, but in an alarming number of cases, it is due to the total *physical* absence of Dad. Toward whom then shall we point the young man who feels he has no one at all? What about the young man who has no one to talk to, no one to understand and confirm him, no one to reach out to, no one to spend time with, no one to help him get through this rigorous style of life called "manhood"? We cannot assume that the nuclear family is commonplace. Not every young man has someone to "steal away" to.

The holy Father knows all too well how vitally important it is for a young man to have an assigned seat among other stable, secure, Spirit-filled and Spirit-led men. Who among us can turn our backs on the great number of men who do not have fathers "to steal" away to, nor sons to nurture? In view of this shortage of available men, the need for different strokes is making a loud call for different folks—namely, the brotherhood at large—to respond. A teenage boy cannot "steal away" to someone who simply is not there. He cannot develop a bond with a biological parent who does not physically exist. When the adolescent heat is turned on, he will have to turn this phase of his life over to the society that has been called to reach out to him when he reaches out to it—the Church. I have conducted men's retreats, brotherhood conventions, and fathering seminars across the nation on an annual basis for the past ten years, and it has never ceased to amaze me what a difference a paternal figure at this stage of life makes. I have been moved, without fail, by the sensitive spirit that the Lord plants into the hearts of the older brothers for those younger ones whom the Lord reveals as being fatherless. On an average, at least five to ten testimonies per annual meeting are culminated with testimonies of men who have freely approached younger brothers and have offered to be their fathers, for as long as they needed or wanted one. Every sanctified muscle in my body pleads mercifully that each baptized believer would realize and appreciate the height, the depth, the inwardly gratifying impact of this kind of on-the-spot, Spirit-compelled adoption.

Try this exercise in conversation with a young man whom the Lord perhaps has placed upon your heart to nurture: Replace his proper name with the expression, "Son." Watch his entire countenance light up when instead of saying, "I'll see you at the Friday Evening Fellowship,

Mike," you will say, "I'll pick you up for Friday Evening Fellowship, and afterward, I'll let you try driving home, Son." Why, if I were a betting man (and I'm not), my wages would stand pretty high on this one. Men, the fatherly faculty and potential within us is nothing short of phenomenal! God made us that way. He has given us the kind of natural influence for nurturing other young men as He has given wives for praying their husbands through the six stages of manhood. Unless we take this initiative immediately, what will become of the upcoming generation? It will not survive. I cannot restate that any stronger—It will not survive! Junior Deacons, Junior Ushers, Sunday School Class students, and Male Chorus recruits are dynamic places and opportunities for young men to sit under older, seasoned brothers. But count up the cost. When they turn 16, what do they do? They lose interest and they leave the church. What's the cost of that gain? Don't repeat it, we can't afford it. If a teenager cannot find what he's looking for at the time that he needs it, in the place that he's in, the *man* in him is not going to procrastinate. While his body is adjusting to changes, his mind will wander straight through the sanctuary doors into outside trouble.

Jacob's grandsons from his second to last son Issachar, turned out to be men of understanding, full of knowledge of the times to know what Israel ought to do. The men of understanding of these times will be proved to know that when God begins to move and reveal the prevailing power of His right hand and how He has shaped the annals of humanity with His discipline of men as leaders, things will have to change. And there will have to be men who will know that what we used to laugh about in the locker room just isn't funny anymore. Our boys aren't surviving past the legal age to marry. They're being destroyed before our very eyes. I can't bear to watch it any longer. My soul asks this question: Is there anyone that you have enough room in your heart for to embrace with your experience for fathering? If you already have two natural sons, do you have room enough if your life for a third one? A spiritual son? Can you look around and ask yourself, "Is there anything in me that can help someone else? (What a thought!) Could you get used to being called, "Dad" by a young man who is not your own? Brothers, I'm pausing here to make an appeal to your heart. I'm appealing to your anointing for bodybuilding...that is, building the Body of Christ with young men who will make a difference. I *know* you have what it takes. (If I didn't, there wouldn't be a Chapter Five.) In all honesty, do you know at least one struggling young man that can benefit from the wisdom, character, and qualities that you have developed from your own daily walk with Christ Jesus? Can you give someone everything that your Dad gave you? Or better yet—everything that he didn't know how to give you? If you can make a difference in a young man's life, then shall:

> *...the Sun of righteousness arise with healing in his wings; ... And He shall turn the heart of the fathers to their children, and the heart of the children to their fathers...* (Malachi 4:2,6).

If not, then tonight the Almighty Father may very well remove me from the picture and ask you face-to-face, "Why not?"

**The Well-Balanced,
Spirit, Soul and Body**

Chapter Five

Two Out of Three
Ain't Bad, Or Is It?

During the first few years after my wife April and I were wed, she worked evenings. I worked during the day. Because she was accustomed to being alert during late evening hours, on her days off she would initiate what seemed to me to be nightlong conversation as she wanted to stay awake and talk. What she really wanted, although I didn't realize it at first, was ministry. I thought, *How do I minister to my wife at three o'clock in the morning?* One evening after worship service, I posed the question to a circle of brothers who had been married longer than I. To my total surprise (and disappointment), their ignorant response alluded to the question of "How could I not know what to do with a woman at three in the morning?" While they collectively burst into fits of hysterical giggling, I discovered that there was a real problem manifesting itself here. There was absolutely no quest for insight into the deeper calling of the spirit man. That's when I knew something significant was out of sync. These brothers, all of whom were well-seated in the Kingdom, were afraid to enter into the depths of their own spirit. They were apparently frightened by the idea of being brought into contact with the power, balance, and manly image of God in them.

As a student of psychology at the time, I was familiar with methods for dissecting behavior into branches so that I might understand how the whole person functioned. After such an experience, I immediately became aware that there is a trembling imbalance in the border of man's soulish, physical, and spiritual natures. When the spirit component of man is in disarray, the image of God in him is distorted and the fulfillment of His purpose for us is set at risk. This danger zone extends all the way down to our hope for healing, recovery, and deliverance. Therefore, until we study man's spirit, we will be ignoring the indispensable element of the human whole.

Quite accurately, the entire individual of man has been distinctly surveyed in Holy Scripture. If we rightly divide the words of the apostle Paul in First Thessalonians 5:23, it will become impossible to disregard those terms that are frequently thought to be psychologically restricted. The conscious, the mind, the temperament, and the will are clearly listed as the elements of man. Paul states, "I pray God your whole spirit and soul and body be preserved blameless unto the coming of our Lord Jesus Christ" (1 Thess. 5:23b). With accurate analysis, we find that man consists of spirit, soul, and body. The outstanding fact of this is that the spirit of man is the main rudder of the life of man. In so many words, "the spirit of man is the candle of the Lord, searching all the inward parts of the belly" (Prov. 20:27).

Although the soul and body may serve to maintain man's affairs on an average level, unless the spirit of man be joined with the Father's, he will not realize nor be able to control what is going on within him on a higher level. This is to say that the spirit of man should rightfully be in the uniquely higher position. Man's spirit, soul, and body come to a balance when the Holy Spirit is melted into the higher of the three—the spirit. We know spirits are transferable, likewise is the anointing. It is the anointing that grant us the rite of passage into the family of Spirit-filled brothers who can reach beyond the temporal tangibles of life and reverently feel who God is. The man who takes control of his entitlement to cojoin his spirit with the Spirit of the Father gets on with the business of his life and proceeds onward to the fulfillment of the greatest advantages of his manhood. Meanwhile, the soul and the body are depending upon the spirit's transformation to the mind of Christ so man might abide under the character of holiness and wholeness.

Observably, the incentive here is threefold: (a) The Holy Ghost uses the Word to tune the spirit, soul, and body of man by piercing, dividing asunder, and equipping him with power (Heb. 4:12; Eph. 6:17). This is done so that he might live, obey, love, serve, and worship God freely. (b) In turn, the spirit of man counterbalances the body and soul so they can act as the limbs through which man's behavior, love, service and worship is carried out. And (c), the anointing of the Holy Spirit seals each stage of each adjustment.

*For what man knoweth the things of a man, save the spirit of man which is in him? even so the things of God knoweth no man, but the Spirit of God. Now we have received, not the spirit of the world, but the spirit which is of God; that we might know the things that are freely given to us of God. Which things also we speak, not in the words which **man's wisdom** teacheth, but which the **Holy Ghost** teacheth; comparing spiritual things with spiritual* (1 Corinthians 2:11-13).

First, with respect to the heart of man, manhood's pressures challenge his soul from every angle. I speak of the type of pressure that disables a man from admitting to his own weaknesses. In spite of such, because our High Priest, Christ has already encountered these pressures, there's really nothing at all wrong with silently praying and pleading your case to Christ in the midst of those persons who antagonize your weaknesses. Brothers, have no fear and don't ever feel embarrassed to say to yourself, "They may shun my company, they can reject my fellowship, just so long as Jesus knows that I don't want to be this way. Public opinion doesn't matter to me anymore. Criticism, rebuke, and condemnation '...hath broken my heart; and I am full of heaviness: and I looked for some to take pity, but there was none; and for comforters, but I found none' (see Ps. 69:20) I care not what your opinion is, just let it be known that I don't want to be this way. I don't want to be afraid anymore to admit that I am spiritually weak because I haven't left enough room for the power of God to bring balance to my character. An honest heart God honors, mends, strengthens, and justifies with deliverance by His Spirit (1 Cor. 6:9-11). All that matters is that my Savior knows that I don't want to be this way." Admittedly, this is hard at times, even awkward. It's quite uncomfortable thinking about things that you haven't learned to say.

With men, you'll always know when you have said the wrong thing because pride often builds a wall of unforgiveness. The damage is done. And when men (especially men) become offended, somehow, the opportunity for forgiveness seems to be the very last option to be extended. That's why bonding among men has been historically unsuccessful. By the way, male bonding should be understood as necessary and biblical (see Ps. 133:1-2). More than being "good and pleasant" isn't this the liberty that God has chosen for us anyway? Isn't this the duty of man toward man? Did not Jonathan love David more than the love of a woman? (2 Samuel 1:26) Is it not the Father's desire that we reach out for one another and loose each other's heavy burdens, let the oppressed go free, and break every yoke? (see Is. 58:6). If we fulfill this duty among ourselves God will cause us to ride "upon high places of the earth" and feed us with "the heritage of Jacob [our] father" (Is. 58:14). And our fellowship shall be complete.

It cannot be overstressed that this phenomenon must first become a Spirit to spirit issue. For a moment, take careful notice of how much man can conceive versus how little he can articulate. Man can conceive wanting to bond with the brethren, but his spirit cannot bring him to say, "Will you be my brother?" He can conceive wanting to share quality time with his son, but he cannot bring himself to say, "Son, it's important that we are friends."

Moreover, many of us have trouble saying, "God I love You" although we probably have an earnest passion for Him. It's hard to get the words out because we're taught to understand love in only one way. But the anointing legitimizes our intimacy with God by discharging into us a holy unction to become open and honest. Deservedly, the man who walks in true relationship with God is invited to commune with facts about God too awesome for human understanding (see Ps. 4:3-4). Men need to know just how complete being *complete in Him* really is.

Needless to say, beyond surviving the dreaded hernia or nicking ourselves while shaving, the circumstances we have in common as men have not presented any major physical problems that outweigh the experiences of our souls, and certainly not our spirits. Among the soul's qualities of reason, understanding, memory, will, and affection, we might also expect to find feelings of loneliness, emptiness, or sadness. And while we're dealing with the real man, what about the age-old emotion of sexual passion? What about it? Where does it fit in? Passion in this sense is experienced in the soul and body. Depending upon how spoiled we are, we as men usually want what we see. When we cannot have what we want, our *spirit* becomes annoyed.

The mouth salivates, the soul palpitates, but the spirit is what must endure the anxiety of having to make the final decision. There is a living reality in godly relationships that maximizes the threefold principle above: When a man's body arrests him at the sight of a woman's utter beauty, it is the spirit of man that is capable of lifting him up and away from the moment by placing him into a realm of safety. Often a man's passion is so strong that his mind causes him to begin pretending as if the emotional pull is not actually happening. This kind of inner warring is not healthy at all. Note, it is not the sexuality of woman herself that makes man complete. Temporary solutions are quickly outgrown. The intimate attraction between man and woman remains free from lust when a man looks at a woman through the dignity of the Holy Spirit. In doing so, he will (get this): adore her with his eyes, verbally complement her beauty, remove his jacket to cover her bareness, then consummate the covenant by bathing her in the oil of anointing (see Ezek. 16:7-9). Great is the Lord!

There is no interaction more awesome than the seal of God's Spirit upon man's spirit. There is no physical or emotional connection that runs deepr than this. We are careful to protect this important interaction and connection because deep within the character of man's spirit, fears, doubts, and untold secrets are bound to become settled. After settling (and rotting), they usually intimidate the stability of the body and soul. Combinations of these secret problems breed needless guilt and shame.

Our young boys, for example, are in danger of being ridiculed on playgrounds by bullies who do not understand why they are caring, gentle, loving, and proper. Of course, it is because they are learning what they are taught from their early experiences with God. The physical boy is seen as a boy, but his young spirit manifests itself in a socially unacceptable weak manner. Society calls it "effeminacy." Make no mistakes, boys who are consistently called "effeminate" or "Momma's boys" grow up with low self-esteem and will suffer with a lack of identity. This syndrome will last in the life a young man for as long as he is without an impartation of an anointing to seal-off his "soft" tendencies.

This does not qualify him for ridicule; for He is still God's property. When he learns (as we all must) to walk in the anointing, he will assume the testimony that the Spirit sets him completely free. "Now the Lord is that Spirit: and where the Spirit of the Lord is, there is liberty" (2 Cor. 3:17).

Today teenage and young adult brothers, who like Jacob are terrified by their own effeminate demeanor are looking for a special touch from the Father to affirm that they are true men within. A thriving indwelling of the anointing will outwardly demonstrate a positively manly spirit, and the shame will die. And once God covers your shame with His abiding love, He doesn't want you to even bring it up anymore. It's over. When the Lord God says you can drop it, drop it! (See Ezekiel 16:62.) To all of you "Jacob's" as you learn to walk in the anointing, stay there. Don't come out.

God will intervene. He will let your brother, and anyone else who may have pushed you aside in the womb, know what it's like to live with shame for a while. In case you don't know who that includes, it includes "every one of the mount of Esau.... For thy violence against thy brother Jacob shame shall cover thee..." (Obad. 1:9b-11).

Again, look at brother Jacob, a disappointment to his father, a deceiver in disguise to his twin brother, a man looking for approval anywhere he could find it. Yet he treasured God's presence in such a special way that when he awakened from his dream of a ladder set upon the earth, he anointed his pillow. By faith, he received the promise that the very land where he laid his head was blessed (Gen. 28:12,18). Jacob had every intention of returning to that anointed place, and he did. When he returned to that consecrated place, God met him there and spoke a word of confirmation into his life by reminding him that he was surely a changed man. (See Genesis 35:1-10.) Is there anything man should hope to do in the Kingdom without first symbolizing the gravity of the anointing? Is there anything he should aspire to become in life without at least somehow acknowledging the anointing's significance?

Truthfully, how many of us are secure in our place in God, but don't seek to go higher in Him because we know cannot do it without the anointing? Is there shame over the fact that we fail to walk with Him to begin with?

Could it be that we feel ashamed and guilty because we have not earnestly sought after His fullness? Or we feel he is absent? Of course He is here! What we desire is His warm, close presence (see 2 Cor. 1:21-22). To suppose that we are not anointed casts upon us the yoke of assault. For God has delivered us of many secretive conditions and sealed our deliverance with a fresh refilling, but in our hour of temptation, our natural sense of doubt causes us to ask ourselves if we are *really* delivered and filled. But the anointing confirms our deliverance and destroys the yoke of assault by bringing out our strengths and hiding our weaknesses where we once hid our faces when we were too ashamed to face God. His power is truth and not a lie (see 1 Jn. 2:27).

How excellent to consider the fruit of the Spirit of God dwelling in the spirit of man. All of these questions grow out of common everyday emotions. But it is supremely the Spirit of God that answers and orders the spirit of man to produce the fruit of love, joy, peace, longsuffering, gentleness, goodness, faith, meekness, and temperance—for the purpose of a balanced godly walk. With respect to the virtues it brings forth, we may safely conclude that the anointing further releases the spirit of excellence in us.

After all has been said and done, tonight when the Lord's Spirit speaks to your spirit, your spirit is going to either reply or resist. Although your soul has been restored and your heart put back together again, when the Lord asks you tonight what He can do for you so that you will be complete in every part—perfectly sound—your spirit is going to have to reply. For some of us, it's time to admit to God that our spirits need to be tranquilized. As for others, our spirits are starving for a serious revival! In either case, all of us need the anointing to complete the job. Which of us cannot use an outpouring of grace to occupy a sanctified body, a renewed mind, and a whole spirit?

I'm sure you will agree that it is more than "fruitful" just to know that the impartation of God's anointing is being released into our lives so that we might mature into fully balanced men in spirit, soul, and body. The balance of only two elements out of three is not only *bad*, but it could be fatal.

One good breeze of the power from on high makes the difference! Isn't it amazing how all our spirit man needs to release us of self-alienation caused by bitter wounds is a touch! We know from the previous chapter that when a young man clings to his father, often he's clinging for strength and protection from those secret things he may be afraid to tell his father Joseph, Jacob's son.

As also mentioned, because we are given to the love of God's Fatherhood, the heavenly Father strengthens the earthly father by His Spirit to, in turn, move upon the heart of his son. The Spirit-thirsty son may never have to fully expose his weaknesses. Sometimes, fatherless men cannot find such arms in which to weep. Perhaps you have found nowhere to lay your head and perhaps you have been forsaken, hated, and for far too long have lived with a cruel name. You will drink the pure milk of nations and be nursed at the royal breasts of kings. Then you will know that "I, the Lord, am thy Saviour, and thy Redeemer, the mighty One of Jacob" (see Is. 60:15-16). According to the father's promise, the trickle-down effect of the glory of the Lord upon you will be inherited by your sons and their sons. You have the written guarantee of this policy whereby this holy inheritance will forever lead them and lock them into a covenant relationship with God the Father. Not only that but it shall keep them when you, Dad, are no longer there.

> *As for Me, this is My covenant with them, saith the Lord; My spirit that is upon thee, and My words which I have put in thy mouth, shall not depart out of thy mouth, nor out of the mouth of thy seed, nor out of the mouth of thy seed's seed, saith the Lord, from henceforth and for ever* (Isaiah 59:21).

Then the inward man might awaken, walk, and worship in the Spirit. And you shall be complete.

No sooner than we leave room for the Holy Spirit to infuse our human spirit, will His anointing peel away the dead skin of our minds that keeps us spiritually separated from our responsibilities to God. He may then shower upon us a fresh layer of patience and committment full of fire and wisdom that will leave a vapor of integrity and reverence for our sons to follow after.

Now that your spirit man is being treated by the Spirit of God, you should become satisfied enough to move on and ask, "Where do I go from here?" I trust that the anointing submerges your old man, and that as you are renewed in the spirit of your mind, you would put on the new man that is created in true holiness and wholeness (see Eph. 4:24). (That's where we go from here.)

It's not too late for men of any age to turn to God and say, "I need this power to cause the different levels of my inner man to fall into place. So, please plunge me into Your power and let me come forth with a handsome anointing so that the evidence of my relationship with You might bring light to another brother who is going through what I've been through, O Lord. Yes Father, confirm me with genuine affection and give me a heart after You. But let my life and manhood be governed by Your Spirit burning within me. Let it burn with a flame so exhausting that my spirit will wobble, sway, and stagger out of the hidden issues of my mind and into the secret places of the Almighty." What holy drunkenness!

The only question that remains is, "What am I supposed to do when the spiritual sensation wears off?" How do I get from Tuesday to Wednesday? The secret for getting from day to day in the anointing is to simply remember that this power outweighs any physical or emotional pressures that may target and attempt to consume you. For as long as you abide in Him, His Spirit will reign, prevail, and remain alive in you. And just when you think that His holy presence has left you, as sure as your daily walk with God from day to day begins with a fresh new "morning by morning," His mercies will be likewise renewed in you and shall not *ever* abandon or fail you (see Lam. 3:22-23).

And you shall be complete.

Helpful Hints
From the Hebrews

Chapter Six

Where Do We Go From Here? Back to Holiness

Like most of my colleagues, my office wall bears a picture framed text; it reads, "Follow peace with all men, and holiness, without which no man shall see the Lord" (Heb. 12:14). For as long as I could remember, I've always thought of the unique grouping of the words "Follow" ... "all men" ... and "holiness" as enlightening. They became more solid and logical to me as I grew in the Lord and eventually provided me with what I consider a sound definition of when, where, and with whom the rules of life should begin. The face value alone of this favorite Bible verse (which I frequently quoted as an emergency Scripture at Sunday dinner table blessing) helped me to further affirm that men of God should feel equally as responsible for rearing children in the fear of God and His holiness as they would in ministering to souls. In a sense, it is the same. In a much larger sense, the hope of Christianity is resting upon it. Customs characteristic to Judaism are intentionally adjusted in alignment with the very ideals that accentuate righteousness. That is to say that they are founded upon the historical strength of holiness, and such history begets history.

Traditional Hebrew parenting reflects the mutual efforts of fathers and mothers in guarding over their children, and the children, in turn, benefiting from their careful and dutiful nurturing—and at times, sacrifices. Unlike today, crimes against parents were literally unheard of, regardless of contributing circumstances. The reasonable statute of chastisement of children from their fathers begun at birth and lasted until the point of early adulthood. The closer the children grew toward adulthood, the more delicately their parents handled chastisement that could potentially damage self-respect. Physical chastisement, as we understand it, of an adult male child was punishable by excommunication. (How do you like that?)

Much is attributed to Hebrew customs in the home and in social settings. Their lack of tolerance for unrighteousness brought severe consequences for sure, but at the same time it produced youngsters ingrained with self-control and discipline. This is the kind of discipline that is slowly deteriorating in our modern society like rust that was once iron.

Note, also, that Palestinian parenthood adopted the practice of providing home schooling, which began with instruction of the sacred laws and beliefs. The divine truths of God, and the appropriate acknowledgment of His honor as the Ruler of the World were principles instilled into children from the primary learning stages. This elementary scholarship with the Scriptures brings us back to the place of respect that was prodigiously earned by Jesus as He sat in the temple "...in the midst of the doctors, both hearing them, and asking them questions" (Lk. 2:46). As a young Hebrew, our Lord continuing about His manly business of carrying out the will of the Father, "...increased in wisdom and stature, and in favour with God and man" (Lk. 2:52).

I am always grieved to report how society has sadly disregarded the fundamental objectives of training. Whether it be because of our current looseness of morality or the lawlessness of New Age dynamics, there's a fog out there that blinds us from clearly seeing and experiencing the fullness of God's family plan. If we were to backtrack a few centuries, we would discover that somewhere along the modern road to solutions, man has been sidetracked from imparting into his children an understanding of the holy thoughts of God; namely the first commandment stipulated with a promise (Eph. 6:1-3). From the very beginning of recorded history, the Torah (religious literature of Judaism) has made a loud and clear statement to man—the appointed head of the family: Hear this My people; this is the way it's supposed to be, and this is the way to govern your household, and this is how I expect you to raise your chilGen (see Deut. 4:9; 11:18-22; Gen. 18:19). I submit, in brief, that until God's Word be adhered to and God's plan for longevity of life for our children, and for our parents, for equality of life begins in the cradle, and with the Word of God—until these Scriptures be followed, until men become men of God, regardless of title—we will not experience the abundant delight that God can cause to be felt from room to room, throughout the home.

Children of the Hebrew household are furthermore instructed to be heedful, that unseemly behavior casts less of a reflection upon proper home rearing and family integrity, but it is a great embarrassment upon the style of godliness as a respectable way of life. These accurate yet brief insights and looks at Jewish customs, history, and scriptural direction, provide an illuminating impression of how the confusion brought on by current liberalism can be disentangled by the example of ancient God-fearing tradition. Traditionally, the day after a Hebrew boy celebrates his thirteenth birthday, he is then at the point of entry into adult male responsibility." The bar mitzvah is proud to acknowledge His heavenly Father in this context of dealing with unrighteousness as the *only* way and hope for man's evil nature:

> Our Father in Heaven, You know that man's inclination is evil from his youth—that it is a fire and we are mere flesh and blood. Observe us in our distress, for we are dust. And see that without You we are nothing, abandoned—only You are the salvation,

for we have no King, help, or support but You (*Bar Mitzvah: Its Observance and Significance*, p. 144).

The ceremonial Jewish bar mitzvah is, in my earnest observation, commendably more than a traditional rite of passage into adulthood, but it is literally a "hands-on" indoctrination of the path, plan, and design of God for man and his descendants. It confirms the testimony that whatever image a man assumes, the laws through which it is achieved have been purposed by God. Becoming an adult meant assuming the responsibilities of performing the commandments and walking in the fear of God Who is holy. *Yam Shlomi, Bava Kamma* 87:37 reads,

> There is no greater festive meal in commemoration of a mitzvah than that which is tendered to give praise and thanksgiving to God that a child has been priviledged to become a bar mitzvah...and his parent has been privileged to raise him to this point and to bring him into the covenant of the Torah.

Observe the structure, order, and family posture: When a boy is named a *bar mitzvah*, his candidacy and subsequent consecration as such proceeds exclusively by the authority and determination of his father. No further substantiation is needed. Therefore, it is inspiring to verify the authority of paternal prediction that a Hebrew boy is a *bar mitzvah* when his father says so, and *because his father said so.* Moreover, the young male's home trained him not to wait until it was time to go to the temple to prepare his heart and mind for worship. His home worship experience and verbal affirmation of his devotion to God fulfilled the requirement of rendering the fruit of his lips.

The mature role, however, for the mature "man" or "woman" by law, was seen in his honor for God as a doer of the Word. Formal, verbal expressions of thanksgiving were pinpointed passaged for the boy who would now enter into manhood:

The *Prayer for the Bar Mitzvah Boy,* begins,

Master of the Universe, I now come before You with great joy since You have sustained me and allowed me to reach this time of life. How glorious is this day in my eyes, as I enter into the category of bar mitzvah, obligated now to perform all Your commandments. All this gladdens my heart and raises my self-dignity.

But I am also delightful to learn through Your servants, the Sages of Israel, that when a Jewish boy reaches the eve of his fourteenth year he is infused with a righteous spirit. It is also accompanied by a yetzer tov, Good Inclination, which assists me in praising Your name. May it be blessed and exalted beyond all blessings and psalms; all in order to fulfill the wishes of our Father in Heaven—for all this we thank You (*Bar Mitzvah: Its Observance and Significance,* p. 148).

In Christianity, our rightful place in the family of man is validated by our adoptive place as children of a holy God. Fluctuating self-identification eventually places shackles of confusion upon us whereby we become bound and psychologically convinced that we belong to no one. But, thanks be to God that we: "...have not received the spirit of bondage again to fear; but ye have received the Spirit of adoption, whereby we cry, Abba, Father" (Rom. 8:15).

An interesting parallel breaks through here: Our own Savior's prayers signifying our adoption hold a profound place in the prayer life of the Jews. Di Sante declares,

The Our Father, of which we have two versions (Luke 11:2-3 and Matthew 6:9-13), also reflects to an important degree the liturgy of the synagogue. Contrary to the claims of [defenders of the faith] who like to emphasize the radical originality of the Our Father, a careful analysis shows that this prayer has deep roots in Judaism (*Jewish Prayer: The Origins of Christian Liturgy*, p. 19).

In keeping with their focus upon godliness, Di Sante further remarks,

We can and must speak of God: we do it by givng names and coming up with definitions, but on one condition: that after saying what we have to say, we have the courage to proclaim him "Holy" (*Jewish Prayer: The Origins of Christian Liturgy*, p. 19).

Israel, God's chosen people, had a chosen path that would lead them into a life style designed for little or no error (Is. 35:8). Having been taught the tenents of the Law from their earliest youth, they carried in their souls and passed down to their children a permanent image of the divine order of God and His commandments—which to them were simply "the rules." Holiness was plainly a way of life. A way of life that believed God to make the crooked straight and the rough places plain so that the utter glory of the Lord might be revealed and so that all flesh might see ti together (Is. 40:4-5).

Despite the small contrasting details that divide our faith from theirs, with maturity we must celebrate this pattern of life that took the time to prepare its young for both the natural and customary readjustments of growing up. Altough psychological and emotional changes occurred first, early adolescence was denoted by a spiritual shift in dependence from the mother to the father (as observed in

Chapter Four). These ordered steps of a young man's nature, although steep at times, led to his greatness as a God-fearing son of God. Because these steps are steep, he is, of course, bound to fall a few times.

An extracted writing of Rabbi Yitzchok Hutner entitled "Fall You Must," reads,

> There is a mistaken and damaging tendency to focus on our great Torah leaders in their mature years. In so doing, we skip their years of struggle to become great; it is as if they emerged from the womb as accomplished scholars and tsaddikim.
>
> We marvel at [their] purity of speech, but who knows about his battles to tame the normal Evil Inclination, of the inevitable struggles and defeats that are part of growth and advancement?...Know, my beloved that the root of your soul is not in the tranquility of your Good Inclination, but specifically in the war against the Evil Inclination. In English the saying goes "lose a battle and win the war." Surely you have failed and you will fail again...and on many fronts you will fall wounded. But I assure you that after the loss of all the battles, you will emerge from the war with a crown of victory on your head...The wisest of all men said, The righteous man will fall seven times, but will arise (Proverbs 24:16).
>
> Fools think that this means...even though he will fall, nevertheless, he will rise. Wise men know well that the meaning is just the opposite: that the nature of his rise is *because* of his "seven downfalls" (*Bar Mitzvah: Its Observance and Significance*, p. 25).

Behold, it is the righteous man, the obedient and doctrinally committed man who will fall seven times, but will rise. In growing up, young men, like the Little League batter who fell and scraped his knee in Chapter Two, your failures will play as great a role in your identity shaping as will protective mentoring. Therefore, as we advance toward a clearer understanding of how our struggles are incorporated into our total man, we shall not be affected to the point of denouncing our allegiance to the law, even if it be upon the painful bruise of our "eighth fall." As soon-to-be victors we will say, "I shall not be removed from the foundation of holiness!" Even the outspoken influence of social values and temptations cannot offer an acceptable reason to compromise the upstanding demands of the law. Our eyes shall not behold the Father's glory in the heavens, except it be fixed upon His holiness upon the earth. (See Hebrews 12:14.)

As stated in Chapter Three, the ark of the covenant was brought into the city by David to restore holiness. Those who will enter into covenant will vow to teach their children the Father's ways so that they may inherit holiness. Except the way of the home be the way of holiness, the hope of its descendants shall be threatened by susceptibility to error, unnecessary mistakes, and pitfalls that could otherwise be avoided (see Is. 35:8).

One of my fathers in the gospel, worthy of the title *sage* once remarked, "What parents do in moderation, children do in excess." In the context of the holy covenant, this might suggest that parents who take the name of the Lord God in vain only give their children reason to curse the home in which they live. Parents who only occasionally remember the Sabbath, give their children reason to ignore the Sabbath, altogether. So, in essence, the company of God's grace keeps us in those difficult clauses of the law where we cannot keep ourselves: "For whosoever shall keep the whole law, and yet offend in one point, he is guilty of all" (Jas. 2:10).

The apostle Paul urged the Church to remain worthy of the unmerited favor of grace and its dispensational mercies for a time such as then—and more imminently, such a time as this. He did not at all excuse the righteousness and correctness that was contained in the originial law; The apostle upholds, "Wherefore the law is holy, and the commandment holy, and just, and good" (Rom. 7:12).

If conditions are so bad that we feel we cannot wholly follow it, Paul affirms that this does not mean that the law is not maintainable. He continues, "For we know that the law is spiritual: but I am carnal, sold under sin" (Rom. 7:14). Consider his earlier statement,

What shall we say then? Shall we continue in sin, that grace may abound? God forbid. How shall we, that are dead to sin, live any longer therein? (Romans 6:1-2)

There is nothing unreasonable or outdated about the law. God's requirement for His people, for the family, and for the Church is still to "be ye holy." He has mercifully tolerated our lack of discipline, but He has not changed His requirement. The reason our children have an outlook of holiness as being antiquated is because we have somehow conveniently shelved it. If we are to return to basic home training under the dictates of the Scriptures, we would implant into our children a sense of reverence and obedience for God as the giver of long life to those who are obedient to their parents. God gives the law: "Honour thy father and thy mother" (Ex. 20:12a).

God sanctifies the mind given to holiness:

And the very God of peace sanctify you wholly; and I pray God your whole spirit and soul and body be preserved blameless unto the coming of our Lord Jesus Christ (1 Thessalonians 5:23).

God promises longevity: "that thy days may be long upon the land which the Lord thy God giveth thee" (Ex. 20:12b).

Moving on, the ideal family trend begins with hearing God's decree of holiness:

Sanctify yourselves therefore, and be ye holy: for I am the Lord your God. And ye shall keep my statutes, and do them: I am the Lord which sanctify you (Leviticus 20:7-8).

And executes it in the context of family order:

For every one that curseth his father or his mother shall be surely put to death: he hath cursed his father or his mother; his blood shall be upon him (Leviticus 20:9).

The natural circumstances of life bring enough affliction without a young man or woman having their days cut off by reason of their dishonor toward their parents. The heartmoving testimony to this fact is likened unto a young couple who resided in the outskirts of Baltimore who had spent a year-and-a-half contemplating the ceremonial bar mitzvah of their son, whose battle with leukemia since age 11 was reshaping their entire life. More than anything, Richie, a studying bar mitzvah wanted to take a trip to Israel. His father and grandfather had told him countless stories that motivated and developed in him an appreciation for Israeli culture and the historic features of the Holy Land. Two weeks before the first day of Channukah, they decided to allow the eager soon-to-be-man to participate in a Hebrew Academy tour to Israel for 12 days. Six days into the trip, his parents were contacted on emergency; Richie had developed respiratory problems. Though their command was to send Richie back home immediately, Richie on his end took the liberty to exert his upcoming manhood by insisting that he would not return until the tour was completed. Each of the remaining six days slowly passed with

Richie's parents' final nerves on edge. Upon their arrival at the airport to greet him, an announcment came across the baggage claim area intercom where they were waiting. "May I have your attention: Would those parents scheduled to meet the touring Academy students kindly report to the international flights executive office located south of the check-in counter." His mother said, "I'll go. You wait here for Richie."

About that time, a distinguished looking grey-bearded man approached Richie's father with the words, "If you're waiting for your luggage, it's going to be a while. This is my third trip to the near east, and it always takes forever for your luggage to come through."

"I understand. I've experienced this wait several times, myself. How was the flight?"

"It was fine. However, I'll never forget this trip."

"I said the same thing, the first time I went to Israel," while scanning the waiting area for his son.

"Actually, it wasn't the trip to Israel that made this vacation worthwhile, it was the trip home from Israel."

"Really? What happened?" Richie's Dad asked.

"A young fellow sat next to me during the return flight. He talked to me. He reminded me of a full-grown man. He had a nature and style about him. He seemed to know what in life was important. He struck up the conversation. He was confident, sure of himself, well-defined. There was something in him that served as a launching pad for a fulfilling life. He possessed good judgment. I can't describe it, Sir.

"Please, go on."

"I asked him why he had traveled to Israel. He gave me the most remarkable answer. 'Because Israel is who I am.' I never got tired of listening to him. He looked out of the window into the blue skies as if he were looking for a Higher Being and said, 'You know, I was on punishment two weeks ago and I was afraid I wasn't going to be able to go. I told my father I was sorry for what I did, but I was still grounded because I didn't admit the *real* reason why I got into trouble. My Dad said that living with secrets is like not living at all, and that God has a way of getting the truth out of every man.' Then he began to tell me about his special ceremony to take place next year. 'I'm trying to memorize something very important, you see.' He said, slipping me a worn-out paper scroll that he had written upon. 'I have to get my last words together. I have to get these last lines right. I can't make any mistakes on this part. Stop me if I make a mistake.' He recited a prayer. I had never heard anything like it. It was so personal, so appropriate."

The older gentleman paused to swallow what seemed to be an enlarging lump in his throat and continued, "He was so convicted about what he was praying. Then he fell asleep. When the plane landed, he wouldn't wake up. What could there possibly have been in a boy of *that age* that could cause him to inspire the life of a man *my age*?"

When the elderly man looked up, seemingly for an answer, Richie's dad was gone.

Had this young sincere soul survived his illness, he would have had the privilege of publicly praying the inheritance of God's holy favor and bounty into the lives of his father and mother. On the occasion of his bar mitzvah, he would have ended the honorable bar mitzvah prayer with the words he had drilled into his own heart:

And from Your blessings, may the house of my father, my shepherd be blessed. May his days be extended in goodness and his years in pleasantry. His efforts should not be in vain.

His offspring should bring him happiness and my mother should take pleasure in her progeny, when they see my perfection in character and perspective...May the expression of my mouth and the thoughts of my heart find favor before you, Hashem, my Rock and my Redeemer (*Bar Mitzvah: Observance and Significance*, p. 140-150).

Instead, these immortal words culminated his life. Where else could we go from here except to the righteousness of the Lord? Though the parents in this parable outlived their son, they can stand blamelessly before God for having raised him to love his faith and to make it his personal career to preserve it.

The strength of families is deteriorating, the minds of our children are being infiltrated with unorthodox propositions, marriages are dissolving, and judgement is coming down because "boys" aren't growing up. It is never too early to establish a life style conducive to holy living. In fact, learning holiness while a "boy" fits more easily into his nature than adopting or being forced into it as an adult man. When the appropriate time comes for we as parents to place building blocks of life into our children's hands, it would please the Father greatly if we would begin their home learning exercises by having them build upon the words *reverence, truth,* and *godliness.* This is an infallible policy: Tell ye your children of it, and let your children tell their children, and their children another generation that this family is going back to holiness (Joel 1:3).

Inherited Inferiority
and Inhibitions

Chapter Seven

The Ishmael Issue

From time to time, it is good for us as believers of the gospel of Jesus Christ to journey across the borders of our faith to appreciate the customs of the nation for whom it first came (Rom. 1:16). Having seen how the Hebrew heritage indoctrinates the minds of their young with loyal esteem for their parents, one can never cease to be amazed at how a child could actually suffer from such a respectable pledge of honor.

One day while meditating on Jacob's personal pain and inhibitions, I entered into prayer and asked the Lord, "Why was so much pain present in Jacob's life?" To my surprise the Father didn't answer with information; but instead, He answered with instructions. I was told to go back to the Scriptures and research the family. To my absolute surprise, the unfolding was nothing short of staggering.

As you will discover in the next chapter, Jacob had an interesting family inheritance. First, on a positive note, he was birthed into the family of the patriarchs. However, after closely examining the text, and backlogging through the brances of his family tree, we know Isaac as his father, but we also note that Jacob's grandfather Abraham had another son by Hagar, his wife's servant. During a brief lapse of Abraham (and Sarah's) faith, it was suggested this servant, Hagar, fill the place that God had specifially reserved for Sarah. The ungodly decision of Abraham to "lie" with Hagar produced a male child named Ishmael, and the manifestation of this action, as we shall see, had far-reaching repercussions. Again, men, observe the sensitivity of a woman. True, the Lord had to challenge their faith with the rhetorical question, "Is anything too hard for God?" But after the confirmation of Isaac, Sarah noticed the playful actions of the boys (Ishmael being the elder) pivotally becoming a bruising experience for her Isaac. This is precisely where we observe the beginning of this adolescent power struggle that left the younger scarred and the elder homeless. Our society today is riddled with the classic example of the big brother visiting too many penal institutions and cemetery plots, as well as substance, sexual, and domestic abuse facilities. How prevalent it is the mark of the "bully" emotions have left some men dysfunctional, victims of tragedy with low self-esteem, and working menial jobs, hating every minute of it, and all along asking only "Why?"

The tragedy that we wish to note is that Isaac's hidden pain from his elder half-brother was still buried without a valve of release. Let there be no oversight in recognizing Isaac's problem. It is now necessary to realize that as a child, Isaac developed his behavioral patterns under the influence of unresolved conflicts of his half-brother and the ungodly relationships of his father. Who can question the valiant display of Abraham's courage when upon Mount Moriah with Isaac? And yet who can doubt that Jacob son of Isaac is now overwhelmed with real pain? What's wrong with this picture? It reflects the subconscious transference of concentrated hurt of a father directly into his innocent son.

Through one good peer into a microscope focused on this family's history, the most chronic feature of a father's soreness bottled-up from childhood into adulthood can be seen in his spontaneous abandonment of his own son, along with the transference of those afflictions that he himself had to endure.

Hence, the Ishmael issue is a roadblock that sits in the way of one's complete breakthrough. It is brought on by a behavior that feeds upon watching others hurt. It takes its root in the shedding of blood where there ought to be a *bonding of blood*. While these associated afflictions break down family peace, it dangerously sows a predisposition of discord into its heirs. The symptoms of the Ishmael complex consist of the badgering, teasing words of a brother that remind you of your own father's imperfections—your own father—the very source of your identity! Consistent patterns of inferior behavior that reveal the "Jacob" in you will arise as a man tonight and claim the victory by boasting that "God will not allow Ishmael's mockery of His sons to go undefended." Yes, sir, those who derive pleasure from making a fool out of any of God's sons are enemies of both God and man, and will be soon cast into the reprimanding hands of the Spirit (see Is. 59:18-20).

How peculiar it is to examine that as we proudly pass down tradition, customs, and values, whatever they be, that we subconsciously pass down pain. Perhaps it is awful enough that our "Ishmael" was not immediately reprimanded for teasing us, but most tragic is the avoidance of the issue that asks, "Why does this pattern continue? Why is it allowed to go on and on? Why?"

Let's not pretend anymore as if nothing happened; it did. Ishmael made Isaac hurt. The pain that was inflicted upon Isaac by his half-brother was passed down to his own son Jacob. Was this due to the fact that this kind of ridicule is embarrassingly difficult to report to our parents? Sarah, the maternally instinctive woman that she was, would perhaps have heard an "I have bruised myself" cry or an "It's not my turn to feed the cattle" cry, but nothing could have matched the sound and apparent anguish that would resonate from an "I don't like what Ishmael said about Daddy" cry. An off-the-wall result of Ishmael's cunning nature dropped a bug in his slick attitude for the perfect place to do his teasing—out in the fields. When you're out in the fields, it seems as if *nobody* can hear you crying.

In American family society when the younger of two brothers cries, seemingly without a reason, mothers and fathers often immediately resolve that they have a "cry-baby" on their hands. Little do they realize the younger cannot bear to repeat the things that are said to him by the older. First, because it only reopens the wound; second, because what's being said is sometimes true. Hurt that has time to settle and mature becomes anger, vengeful anger. And so we pass it on.

Silent cries of fear and abuse have an incubation period that can last from 10 to 40 years—to a lifetime. After 30 years, I finally learned that it is all right for a man to admit that he's been hurt. Regardless of the silent midnight cries that alone could never have rescued me from the childhood anguish of being sexually molested by another member of my own family, I passionately understand how such a difficulty could impair a child's freedom of expression and trust. In too many cases, as in mine, the child never finds a way to get free of the fear long enough to admit it to anyone at a time when it can be dealt with. It's frightening.

Confronted fear, especially in the face of family crises, persistently prompts all kinds of excuses. Excuses for emotional distance toward our sons may start with statements of hero-coward philosophies and end with complete lies. If the truth be known, the emotional distance is another link to the chain reaction of hurt from not having been touched as a child, or having been *touched wrong*. In either case, the scars leave your emotional man frustrated. Acceptance versus rejection in the father-son relationship, believe it or not, carries the potential weight of psychological stability or instability. The deteriorating condition of mankind has brought things to that point. The presence of God, however (bless His name), accepts us and brings us closer to Him. Whenever the trauma goes untreated, it is only because, although God is near "we know it not" (Gen. 28:16).

We *do* know, however, that far too frequently, the individuals who we love the most are the very ones who inflict us most severely. I have no reservation in reckoning that, although he was a half-brother, Isaac actually loved Ishmael and wanted to share with him a full-blooded brother-to-brother friendship. Ishmael's own illegitimacy negatively intruded into the personality of Isaac.

Prolonged effects of labeling, teasing, and ridicule do not silently and innocently escape. They cannot use the closets in which we often hide, nor do they necessarily vanish like a secret that we attempt to conceal. Instead they weigh us down and thump in rhythm with our heartbeat whenever we hear the name of the person who made us this way. Like an experiment, we hear the name (*Ishmael*), experience the signal (*teasing*), and trigger a response (*anxiety*). The spirit of man can endure only so much inherited inferiority before he either collapses into the trust of the Father God Whose merciful love will cover the multitude of faults, or before he casts the same curse upon his own children.

Apparently, experienced and inexperienced child rearers alike have become strangely naive to this fact that children hear and absorb what they are told early in life with a permanent impression. Junior took his first step at the beginning of Chapter Four. Since then we have taken the time with him to carefully watch how his play activities shape his initial learning skills and breed in him a lasting perspective of the world.

Language development, for example, which might employ "Junior's" learning by memory as a teaching tool, could be equally as harmful as it may be helpful: "Good boy, say 'Good boy'; Bad Boy, say 'Bad boy' " is a familiar verbal exercise that shapes the child's perspective of himself as accurately as maliciously continuing on to have him repeat to you, "Love child, say 'Love child,' " The seed of ridicule is thus planted. Where ridicule is planted, the seeds that God have given to the parent to plant and nourish will bud, but will never flourish. This means that the child's predestined inner greatness will never make its true mark upon the world.

Generations of wounded forefathers have been guilty of underestimating the innocent sensitivity of children. Perhaps they cannot read into adult roundtable lingo, but many children *can* most definitely discern the subject matter of family-wide whispers.

Could the pain you distribute rest upon a hidden (or whispered about) tragedy whereby your son is robbed of the right to be named your "pride and joy" because the firstborn son who you prayed for was stillborn ten years ago? And the son who came three years after him, but certainly not after your hurt, survived his delivery but became emotionally destroyed when he learned that he was born into the disappointment of you, his father, who simply never got over the first loss. (But nobody wants to talk about it.) Can't we see what's happening? Or will it take God to show it to us *tonight.*

Have you seen the parallel line of well-meant abandonment and good intention as it occurs upon the path you may have traveled? Perhaps it happened when you were sent away as a newborn to live and be raised by another family within the extended family, merely to avoid the shame your mother would have brought to her parents by having given birth to you out of wedlock. You eventually learned the identity of your real parents but you never learned who the *real you* is. These days, when children ask for the truth, whether they were abandoned, adopted, legitimate, illigitimate, full-blooded or half-blooded, let's do something special for them and tell them the truth. Anything less than that will only pass the curse along and cause pain to continue to prevail.

Pain prevails today because we have been placed in situations that we do not ask to be in. Is it entirely your mother's fault if Dad gave up on life soon after you were born, deserted the home, and left her to raise you without a man's influence and presence? Have you considered that she probably didn't know that it wasn't a healthy behavior or in the interest of your boyhood to be expected to sit in your bedroom politely, play quietly, and not release your drive for instant activity. Isn't it quite likely that she didn't know that this behavior is typically material to what makes you a *normal* boy? Since your boyhood days your outlets became more and more peculiar as you grew older. Friends teased you and the teasing was coupled with words from an "Ishmael" who didn't know where Dad was anymore than you; he just wanted to compound your misery.

Have we paused to really think of how hypocritical it is for us to cry for arms to embrace us with acceptance and understanding without first stopping to think of what kinds of things have been said to our children and what they have been expected to measure up to? That voice of punishment in us that wants them to know what real rejection feels like—so that they will know why we are the way we are—is cutting off our seed. God passed down His love for us through His Son. Man has not elevated his mind to the point where he can reflect that example. So until he does, let us cling to the Son's experience in the face of infirmity. Inscribe it upon the table of our hearts:

> *For we have not an high priest which cannot be touched with the feelings of our infirmities; but was in all points tempted like as we are, yet without sin* (Hebrews 4:15).

The point here is not *infirmity*, it is not *temptation*, and it is not *sin*. The point here is the wondrous assurance that we have *a high priest*.

Unlike Isaac, who had a half-brother who inflicted pain, we have an older Brother who has come to remove the pain. He loves us and understands our fears, our insecurities, as well as our illegitimate hangups. We have a High Priest! Isaac had a half-brother who was driven by a spirit of ridicule. Notice the juvenile manner of Ishmael's harassment of Isaac; by provoking the issue of "whose daddy committed what with whom": The only thing he proved was his own distant understanding of their father, Abraham.

Let's take this from the beginning: Ishmael teased his half-brother Isaac and inflicted pain upon him. When Isaac grew up, he in turn named his son "Jacob" (Deceiver), made him hurt, and thus Jacob inherited the pain of his father. When Jacob grew up, he raised boys so sharply affected by the curse, that they sold their younger brother into Egypt, causing the young Joseph to hurt and to inherit *three generations of pain!*

Are you disturbed about something that you can't seem to put into words? Has it been with you for so long that it has started to hurt? Is it possible that you have inherited someone else's pain? Whose pain did you inherit? Whose namesake are you? Let me ask that again, whose *namesake* are you? Hold that thought because something interesting happens here.

As beloved as he was by his father, Joseph the son of Jacob still felt the infirmities of his forefathers and the liberties they took in acting out their inherited complexes. His brothers' spiteful behavior toward him reminded him of the curse every time Jacob showed Joseph how much he loved him. How pitiful it is when a boy can't enjoy his father's love because there's a family curse standing in the way. However at the point of mourning over the death of their father, Joseph fell upon their father's face, wept over him, and returned to Egypt. There he stood face-to-face with his brothers who feared that he would hand down to them the family scar. Joseph, the "fruitful vine" of the family, gloriously put an end to the madness and said, "As for you, ye thought evil against me, but God meant it unto good" (Gen. 50:20a). It's over. It stops right here. I'm not going to curse you. Instead, I will, from this day, help and save this situation from going on any further. It's gotten out of hand. I will embrace you with love and not hate because I want to recover, to repair, and restore us to family life the way it was intended to be. You don't have to be afraid, you don't have to feel inferior or be inhibited any longer. I will nourish you and your children and be kindly affectionate towards them (see Gen. 50:20-21). I vow to correct the traditional family tendency and heal the family pain by instilling love and understanding and by establishing a circle of brotherly trust upon the promises of Jehovah, so that the healing might remain throughout the lives of our children to come.

God honored Joseph with longevity; he lived to see his children, grandchildren, and great-grandchildren, all of whom were brought upon his knees (Gen. 50:23). Joseph the curse-breaker blessed the Lord and his seed in turn was blessed from generation to generation.

Are you prepared to break the curse tonight, and admit to God what Ishmael did to you? Are you tired of being empty and alone in your search to please God? Are you so tired that you will openly disclose to Him who it was that hurt you *the most*?

If not, then *tonight...we wrestle*.

**Getting the Boy Out
of Us Is a Man's Job**

Chapter Eight

Tonight, We Wrestle

Well, brothers, it's been a hectic day for us. But it's not quite over yet. It's time for God, as promised, to reveal to us how He intends to get to the bottom of these issues.

The divine revelation is opened with the scene of God meeting Jacob. Jacob is a man perplexed in his growth and troubled on every side by the experience of having lived up the label his father gave him at birth. Again—for your own soul's sake— do not hear "Father, I stretch my hands to Thee; no other help I know" as a spiritual cliché or a routine prayer-starter. Rather hear it and speak it as the first step toward rightfully receiving from God what you have been crying out for all of your life—to pastors, deacons, teachers, coaches, girlfriends, and spouses. Speak it all to Jesus! Let go of those repressed issues, and watch the promise of your peace come to pass. Give it to the Father of daily mercy Who was there all the time, though you knew it not (see Lam. 3:22-23; Gen. 28:16). You "knew it not" because of your inherited inhibitions, strong-willed expectations, unexpressed needs, and unrequested healing. Our indirect, evasive, dishonest answers to the question "My son, what's wrong?" have actually distracted many of us from His holy, loving, caring, healing, problem-solving presence.

When the Father shows up in the midnight of your life, He's not coming to discuss sports, politics, or business. He comes to break down your inner-warring and to bring your emotions back into peaceful order; to wrestle out of you tears of truth; to fix that fatherhood fear and all its accompanying anguish; to send you back to sleep just before daybreak, only to reawaken you to the covenant-binding clause of *joy* that comes in the morning (see Ps. 30:5).

Tonight, come before Him and face this potentially degenerating dilemma with a *confident* openness that cries out, "I'm a man who *can't,* but you're a God who *can.*" Fathers, when your child enters his first day of school and is asked by his teacher, "What is your name?" face it, your child's answer is going to be a reflection of you. When your children must mourn your death the texture of their tears will either bring back precious memories, painful experiences, or perhaps bittersweet peace as a combination of them all. But before the first grain of dirt covers your body, an image—a very real, obvious, apparent image—will be etched into the heart and mind of your children who may still carry far too many unanswered questions of how and why they turned out the way they are.

That is why the Father comes to us at this hour; for the purpose of rescuing us from sinking into devastation. As we cry out through our behavior (or cry inwardly, as the case may also be) for a touch, for a resolution to our emptiness through His blessed contact with the inner man, He offers us a glimpse of the victory ahead. It's called *grace.*

Grace, as we know and appreciate it, is freely given through God's special influence upon the heart, and will grant us person-to-person comfort with God, starting tonight. *Tonight, we wrestle*—tonight, now, today, at this very moment in time. We don't have any more time to waste. We've got to address this situation in Christianity and get it corrected—now or never! The end of time is swiftly approaching. Tonight, we wrestle. Tonight, we hear the question, we face the problem, and we receive the solution, Jesus!

If, after swallowing as much as you can of the previous discussions of Christianity complicated by being given the wrong name, you insist on contending with and consulting the natural sciences before hearing and answering the voice of the Lord—if it makes you happy—you may avoid the issue by exploring the long-term differences between identical and fraternal twins (and seemingly the Scriptures suggest that Jacob and Esau were probably fraternal). It will not matter, nor will it forfeit the ultimate wrestling match. On God's agenda *it's got to happen tonight!* Tonight, whatever situations have locked you into a mode of complacency in turning a deaf ear to the divine call of manhood, the time has come to answer the voice of the Father of Mercy for the survival of the universal Christian body that is bleeding for *real men*—it's got to happen, tonight!

In these final hours we find ourselves tossing and turning with the conviction that on the very surface at least, we cannot help others until we first help ourselves. This is precisely why God with His own persistence declared that He must start with you, Jacob.

Throughout the episodes of this night, we are invited to embrace the presence of Christ-patterned fatherhood, brotherhood, forgiveness, restoration, and peace in our lives. The pursuit of meaningful fatherhood without the experience of meaningful sonship is as stagnant as a builder who lays his foundation upon the sand. (See Matthew 7:26-27.) The hope of this lesson is that after enduring mocking, scorning, rejection, and neglect, this bruised mortal body that hopes for victorious manhood will be resurrected in the name of Jesus!

Often we don't even express ourselves to God as we should, for if we did, it would draw out of us those things that keep us from becoming the men and women that God would have us to be. When our prayer life is transparent, fervent, and effectual, then the voice of God would not seem so distant in asking us, "What's wrong." A transparent prayer comes from a heart that has nothing to hide. As the heavenly Father looks down upon the condition of manhood across the centuries and especially today, He's inviting us to tell Him what's wrong. If only we would open our hearts and let Him in, He would solve the problems and heal the wounds.

Quite apparently, the reason we think nothing is wrong is because our fathers were this way and their fathers before them, and they all survived. That's just it. They survived. But how many of them truly succeeded? God's message of love and deliverance conveys this: "If you earnestly desire to become the man that you have been predestined to become, and as your heart races with thoughts of the past while being interrogated by the question "What's wrong?" let it go and answer Him. Your change is only a heartbeat away!

There are battered women, abused men, neglected sons, and refused daughters in your daily surroundings that are fellow victims. But *this night*, the spiritual and emotional conflicts will be resolved. One of the fears of night is of the darkness it brings. Many of us become paralyzed because we are so dependent on our sense realm, that we forget about our faith in Him who will never leave or forsake us, even in the dark.

Often if we can't see or feel His presence, we automatically assume that the Father is not near, when in fact, nothing could be farther from the truth. In studying the first chapter in the Book of Genesis, we note the evening and the morning were the first day. As a matter of fact, before there was a day, there was darkness.

The Scriptures seem to suggest that God's day begins at darkness, and by the time you see light He has finished (see Lam. 3:22-23). As the night becomes old, all those deep, humiliating, unlawful things that you were too embarrassed to tell anyone will also become old. They will be destroyed in both Heaven and in earth. You will be released from those temptations and obstacles of your life; God said, *"tonight."*

When you confessed the lordship of Jesus Christ unto salvation, you took upon yourself the place in Him that would bring Him back to you to restore you, since you had drifted away. You now have a relationship, and because you have a relationship, there are some elements that cannot remain within your character, behavior, worship, marriage, home, service, and fellowship; *tonight, we wrestle.*

Since it's getting late, allow me to share with you how (and where) it all began: One evening while doing research for a thesis project, I was keenly aware of the fact that the further I investigated, the more painful the information became. It soon became very clear that the Father was addressing issues of my past. These were painful issues that I hadn't managed to resolve. He brought up issues that would challenge the trust of the closest friendships, areas of adolescence that could cause someone to miss the timing of God, and flashbacks of the past that would have trailed anyone into their future.

Finally, after finding myself in a place that could only be described as a hurricane of pain, *I admitted* that I needed the Holy Spirit to minister to me. I could not stay in denial any longer. Then the warm presence of the Father was manifested. The Father then asked me a question. He said, "Son, do you know why Jacob's name was *Jacob?*" In as scholarly a manner as I knew, I flipped through the mental pages of my reliable *Strong's Concordance,* and every familiar reference that I could recall. I came out with the answer, "Lord, his name means 'Trickster, grabber of the heel, deceiver.'" I felt sure that in the middle of this paradox I had at least held my own ground. Within my spirit man, I could hear the alarming sound of godly disappointment. "No", the Father said, "The question was not, 'Do you know what his means.'" He repeated His question, "Do you know why Jacob was named 'Jacob?'"

In the midst of a fearful reverence, I became filled with awe. I didn't understand why inner secrets of my life were being exposed. I was seeking help, and the Lord was asking questions. I was taken all the way back to childhood experiences of abuse and sexual advances. There was the painful delay of my future because of an ongoing heroin experiment began at the age of eleven. Sorrowfully and painfully, I remembered exchanging high school classes for gambling at the pool room. Finally, I was able to confront and unlock some of the most challenging areas of my life with the hope of becoming free from the painful memories of the past, but the Lord wanted to talk about the 'Jacob' in me. I knew that when God speaks, we must answer. It was clear that if He asked a question twice, I must admit I didn't know. Softly, I answered Him, "No, Lord." It was then that a clear impression was made upon my spirit by the voice of the Lord, and the answer rang out clearly, *"Jacob's name was **Jacob** because his father said so."* In His own kind, wonderfully patient way, the Lord made this truth a little easier to accept.

Although weeping uncontrollably and shaking beyond measure, I knew the Father was present to unlock private issues that were too painful for me to discuss openly. But why did He choose this manner? Why ask about Jacob? How did this noble family fit in? Could it be that this great patriarchal family was slightly dysfunctional? Was it true that part of the *Adamic* nature was still at work?

Was I dishonoring the Scriptures by remembering Abraham, the "Father of Faith," with great intentions of trying to assist God in manifesting the promise of a son produced through a bondwoman—a son named Ishmael? My mind was racing trying to put up walls and to avoid remembering that Ishmael teased, taunted and harassed the real seed of promise, Isaac. Undoubtedly these experiences left Isaac with negative memories of his past, and now we observe there came a day when twins were born to Isaac.

I remembered my own experience in the delivery room; immediately upon the arrival of my daughter, the doctors did the necessary medical things and placed her in my arms. Then the question came, "What is her name?" The answer the Father had revealed became so real. Jacob was named Jacob *because his father said so.* Clearly Isaac held them in his arms, looked at one and said, "Esau" (you will be a blessed child, you will advance, you will achieve) and turned to the other and said, "Jacob" (you will be a deceiver, a trickster, a supplanter). Most of us in our Christian walk have heard that Jacob was "Mamma's Boy," but honestly, what child doesn't look for love? Which one of us would not draw closer to the love of another after being innocently born and hearing that your father loved your brother more than he loved you? Can the fact be erased that words produce? The Scriptures specifically record, "In the beginning was the Word" (Jn. 1:1a).

As destiny would have it, God now shows up to change the *word of man,* and release His *word of promise* (see Gen. 25:23).

Like a temporarily spiritually blinded child, I looked into the text as closely and desperately as I knew how, and like a bombshell out of heavens, it leaped upon me from off the page. I trembled fearfully before Him. I was almost drowned by my tears while under the the supernatural outpouring of conviction that arrested my inner man; God gave me a revelation of Jacob's encounter with Him the night they wrestled. It was real. And if the truth be told, it still is. Little did Jacob know, however, that the Father had already planned that night where blessings would flow, and oh, what changes would be made! After looking back through the text, it is interesting to see how Jacob became what he was called by family and others.

I can hear the Lord asking *"what's wrong, My son?"* He is speaking into the dark, lonely emptiness of your feelings of not being loved and carried into the pattern of one hardship following another to the point at which you are ready to sell-out to the adversary and just give up. The Father sees you as you barely lift your feet to walk, as you struggle to open your mouth to give Him an overdue utterance of praise. You're silent from the aching reminders of how bad things really are and how sincerely you pray that they would get better. Your depression gets you up in the morning, drags you around through the day, and brings you back to your pillow for another restless night. But *tonight* God comes to wrestle with you for as long as it takes to deliver you from the things—whatever they be—that hinder you from becoming all that you should.

Imagine Jacob being held by his father and being called *Trickster*. Jacob was not born this way; he became what he was called every day. God intends for those of us who have been designated to carry out His will on earth to live up to His expectations alone. Little did Jacob know at his birth, about God's ability to change names. He was unaware that his patriarchal grandfather was promoted from "Abram" to "Abraham" and his grandmother was elevated from "Sarai" to "Sarah." Jacob was about to collide with a wonderful truth. *God reserves the right to change names for His purpose.* When the connotations of our name pronounce failure into us, we *think failure* and *live failure* until we overhear those secret statements that suggest that we have been unappropriately named (see Gen. 27:36). We shall know that we have been fittingly *re-named* when our new name rings with a tone of destiny like Abraham, who although formerly "Abram," ultimately became the "Father of many nations" (see Gen. 17:5).

The sun is setting slowly, and your soul is tired, altogether tired of everything. Your eyes reveal the irritation, fatigue, and acute tension of not knowing what emotional ills tomorrow will bring. Little do you know that this night His anointing will not lift until you are free. Jesus said, "Come unto Me" (Mt. 11:28). Just as you are descend into the midnight of mercy where the Father waits to set you free. It's midnight in your life, in your home, in your finances. It is midnight, and the Lord appears to you, and compassionately yet omnipotently asks, *"What's wrong, My child?"*

■ 12:30 a.m.

Why aren't you the man that I called you to be? Why aren't you the faithful, praying, Bible-studying, dutiful deacon that I've called you to be?

> Father, it seems as though no one cares. No one sees the works that I do, and the more I do, the less I am appreciated. Besides, no one ever took me, taught me, and trained me.

Jacob, what's the real reason you don't study properly to show yourself approved unto me?

> Well, I'm ashamed because I don't read very well. I remember even in the third grade the other children laughed at me.

■ 1:00 a.m.

Why are you so inconsistent? Why can't you finish things that you start?

> Lord, I spend so much time in Your service that things never balance out long enough for me to really put my mind to more excellent things.

No, Jacob. What's the real reason?

I never had a role model, Lord. My father never took time out to be with me. I never had anyone to look up to or encourage me in my pursuits. I try not to, but I always feel as though someone else can do a better job. It's been hard for me, Lord, but I tried.

Yes, I know. But what else is wrong?

Jacob, I've noticed that you're faithful in attending prayer service. How is it that you can pray for the homeless, yet you omit praying for your own family?

Lord, I have a sure promise that you'll save my children.

Jacob, your spirit bears witness with me that you don't pray for your own brothers and sisters at all. Does the overwhelming truth that each of you have different fathers leave you helplessly embarrassed? Jacob, aren't you aware that I can step into your past and heal the memories of late night visits in your home when you were just a boy? Why can't you trust Me for your deliverance?

I have a hard time trusting *any man*. Men are insensitive, unreliable, and disloyal to true covenant.

But I am not a man that I should lie! What else is wrong?

■ 1:30 a.m.

Why don't you fast when My Spirit pulls at your heart? Even your tithing has become irregular. Why do you only give Me ten minutes of prayer each day? I remember when you would come before Me and seek Me with a broken heart. I want to bring you to a loftier place in worship, but I have not had your attention lately—that's why I'm here—I want to know why, and I shall not be removed until I have straighted out your life: Tonight...we wrestle!

■ 2:00 a.m.

Why don't you worship Me the way you should?

Lord, sometimes I see other women, often very young ladies, that I find myself distracted by.

You have had a relationship with Me all these years, and you still cannot discipline your mind?

Sometimes I just can't help myself.

Jacob? Have you earnestly desired help? Am I not a keeper of perfect peace of those whose mind is stayed on Me? You know that! What else is wrong? Why do you go from job to job and take your family, whose welfare has been entrusted to you, through unnecessary hardships? Why, Jacob, can't you be steady in the workplace long enough to bring forth a reasonable harvest for your home?

I don't like my job. The people are full of envy and prejudice and the promotions are not offered to me, Lord. I'm not sure why. Maybe it has something to do with where I was born, maybe it's the color of my skin, or perhaps it's the neighborhood I live in. I know you see what goes on. I try my best to remain committed to my work.

Why do you mix your failure with your ethnicity? Is there any Black man, White man, any man at all who can block your success? Have I not promised to bless them that bless you and curse them that curse you? I will not fail thee, nor forsake thee? And why is it that you will respect and listen to your boss more often than you will respect and listen to the shepherd I have placed to watch over your soul?

My boss is paying me and helping me to feed my family.

But your pastor loves you, and he's feeding your soul. Is your pastor not the very ordained one who has the rule over you? Are not those who I have placed in rule over you worthy of double honor? Don't inhibit your blessing by not rightly honoring them for their works sake. That is precisely why I continue to show you greater ministry but have not released it unto you. You're not ready for it. That is why I continue to show you elevation in the ministry but have not ordered that it come to pass. You're not ready for it.

■ 2:30 a.m.

(Is it possible for you to put yourself in Jacob's place, only to realize your opponent has a superior advantage over you. His power rules even the night, and His wisdom disallows even the "trickster" to obtain even the slightest edge. Painfully Jacob has to come to terms with the fact that not only is He a merciful God, but also that the Most High rules with a rod of iron (see Rev. 2:27). Jacob's thought process now comes to terms with an interesting predicament: *I can't run away anymore, and I can't lie my way out; yet He's still here and hasn't done away with me.*

What else is wrong? The older you get, the less balanced you seem to be. Don't you know who you are yet?

But Lord, I feel as though I never had a real childhood. There are so many places I've never been and so many exciting things that I've never experienced. I want to know what it's like to try some things.

What kind of things?

Oh, some synthetic medications, products for my anxiety and my nerves, and....

Are you not aware that before a thought could pass through your mind, I know it. It must pass through Me. You are engaging in steady attempts to figure out how you can trick Me when you speak to Me. Are you not aware that I know the very thoughts you think? The reason I showed up is because you are a "trickster"! So, don't jeopardize your blessing by failing to yield to me. Tell Me what you're being tempted with.

One of the fellas offered me something to make me feel better.

You don't want that. You're just tired of hurting, and you have not exercised the slightest measure of faith in My heart-mending love for you. Have you asked Me to take away the pain? You have not! What else is wrong?

I have so many burdens, Lord.

My son, tell Me the real problem. When you see your brothers in Christ hurting in the midst of agony and crisis, why can't you put your arm around them and encourage them by sharing a word to lift their hearts?

Well, Lord, they need to be alone to get a break-through, travail, and wait for their deliverance and....

No. Tell Me the real reason. Tell Me why you can't come out of yourself long enough to bless someone else's life?

Because I'm hurting too. No one ever reached out to me when I was growing up and hurting. My family never thought I was important.

Thank you. You're finally starting to be honest. What else is wrong?

Lord, please, it's almost 3:00 in the morning. Please let me go.

*...and there wrestled a man with him, **until the breaking of day** (Genesis 32:24).*

I'm not finished with you! Tonight, you will tell me every-thing.

But, Lord! I feel better now. Can we stop here?

Tell Me what else is wrong. Why do you reprimand and chastise your boys when they fall down, hurt themselves and cry?

Because boys aren't supposed to cry. I want them to be real men.

No. My son. Tell Me where the underlying discomfort comes from when your boys are releasing painful emotions?

Lord, you know I've had painful emotions all my life, but I've never had anyone's arms to cry into. I had no father to hold me. I had nowhere to bring my heaviness. So I need to be healed, before I can heal them.

Why didn't you take My hand during those times.

You were there all the time, and I didn't know it.

Jacob, I don't ever want to be in your presence again and for you not to know it. You were left alone so that deliverance might be brought into you life. If you are going to reach a lost, perverse, afflicted generation, the healing must begin with you. Now, My son, whether you're ready for tonight or not, I have a divine assignment for you. I'm here because little may you know it, but there are too many things hindering your maturity in Me, and I have come to correct them and put you back on course. You need to obey what's going on in the spirit realm. Now, I want to talk to you. Tell me what else is wrong.

■ 3:00 a.m.

Why are you headed towards your third marriage? I want you to know that the games are over. These issues are very serious to Me.

And another thing (To the sisters who happen to be travailing in hopes of finding answers to hidden pain, the Father is wrestling with your inner being also, and wants to set you free from the unspeakable issues that cause unrest.) *Why, Ms. Jacob, do you compare your husband with other men, when I have blessed the union with the one you have?*

Unfortunately, I can't stop thinking about the first man I ever considered seriously. Lord, I cannot get him out of my mind. Sometimes, I wonder if I should have married him instead.

No, you should not have. Stop blaming meaningless situations from your past and tell Me about those things that you have chosen to hide. What's the problem...the real problem? Why won't you have lunch with Shirley anymore?

Lord, I really think she's a wonderful person; however, the questions she asks at different times become overwhelming. I think she should go to Bible study?

Is it because Shirley works across the street from the abortion clinic? Is it because there's an unsettled issue that won't go away, and you have painful memories of a pre-salvation experience?

Why is it that I can't forget it?

■ **4:00 a.m.**

God, I made so many mistakes in the past. I can't forget them, and I wish the memory of them would just go away.

I know the things of which you speak. I know the things that have kept you bound out of shame and guilt. I know why it's hard for you to face certain people. I also know why it's hard for you to re-establish broken relationships. But I have not come to magnify pain. I am here for your deliverance. The pain is ended. What else is wrong, Ms. Jacob?

Lord, it's 4:30. Won't you please let me go? I don't want to talk anymore.

...and there wrestled a man with him until the breaking of day (Genesis 32:24).

No. I'm not releasing you until you tell me what else is wrong?

I'm not happy with the way that I look, and I'm afraid my appearance—my weight, my shape, and my short hair—are keeping me from being the total woman that I want to be.

What do you want to be?

I just want to be happy, my Father.

How could you, My creation, have adopted the standards that the world has? My dear daughter, who are you trying to impress? Are you suggesting that I made a mistake when I made you? You are fearfully and wonderfully made in My image. I did not make a mistake! Stop entertaining worldly foolishness; use your body to glorify Me! I am a jealous God, and I will not have you falling prey to images, and perceptions and those things that lead to idolatry. Put it away and tell Me what else is wrong? Tell me the real reason why you are constantly over-eating. Why do you eat when you're not hungry? Why do you eat foods that are not fit for your diet?

Lord, you know I've tried everything and nothing seems to work.

I didn't ask you what you've tried, I asked you why you do it? What are you running from when you eat in excess?

My God, my God, I'm tired. I don't want to talk anymore.

(The Lord then turns again to Jacob and says:)

You've been in My presence for five hours. For five hours I have been holding you. But I want you to tell Me what is bothering you most of all.

God, I've told you everything!

Jacob, you didn't tell Me about the time you were molested as a child.

Lord, that was a long time ago. It's over.

Yes, My son. But it's still bothering you. Isn't that the real reason you won't let your daughter go to the mall with friends? Isn't that why you don't allow your boys to affectionately express themselves to you? Yes, old things are passed away, but have you noticed, you can't say "I love you" to your children? You haven't renewed your mind.

■ **5:00 a.m.**

Jacob, what else is wrong? Why haven't you told me about the time incest was committed between you and your daughter?

No, Lord! That wasn't my fault. That was Laban's fault. It was dark, I didn't know what was going on...I thought it was Rachel and....

I didn't ask you whose fault it was, I asked you why you refused to tell Me about it, especially since it has kept you bound for so long. Jacob, why do you always have to put the blame on someone else? Aren't you tired of putting the blame on everything and everyone? Why can't you tell Me, Jacob? I'm here to straighten it out for you once and for all. You won't have to go through this again, but you must come clean of everything, tonight. Tonight is the night, Jacob. Tell Me what's wrong.

(Suddenly, Jacob's life began to flash before his eyes. He saw himself in the midst of struggle after struggle, trying to prove to himself that he was somebody. He saw days and nights spent comparing himself with himself, never satisfied with the success of his life. The games of competition with his brother were over. The lies were old.

The years of deceit were now in the hands of the God of his fathers. The same God who commanded the blessings of his forefathers now pinned Jacob to his ultimate moment of truth. The scenes ended, and as he sighed in despair, he swallowed his last ounce of deceit. In the tone of a newborn baby who pitifully sobs to be picked up and held he whispered "Father?"

Yes, Jacob.

> The real thing that bothers me is that when I was born, my father held me, and said I would be a trickster and deceiver. My father didn't love me enough **to walk with me, talk with me, teach me, encourage me, but instead** he *called me* "Jacob."

(God proudly looked at Jacob, the way his father never looked at him, and said,)

My dear son, you've finally owned up to everything that bothers you.

God was so in love with Jacob that he would not let him go until he was *absolutely, totally, infallibly, and completely clean!* That's what He wants to do in you. Everything had to go. God is saying to *you,* "Tonight, everything must go. The games are over. The cover has been pulled off. You're standing naked before Me. I see your pain. I know your disappointments. I know all the things you've gone through. I understand *all of the things* that make you feel less than a man, less than a woman, less than a son, or less than a daughter. If you would just give it to Me, I will fix it for you."

God is saying, "I know the path you have taken. I was there all the time. Do you remember? I am the *El* which is why I met you at *Beth-El* (see Gen. 28:19). I know you were neglected by your father, overprotected by your mother, labeled by friends, teased by your half-brother, unloved in your home, molested by your uncle, whispered about by your aunt, rejected by your peers, alienated from your dreams, and ignored by your brothers in Christ. I know all about it, and I care. But tonight none of that matters anymore because this evening's confrontation has not been totally about your will. This evening has been about My purpose, My will and My promise for your life. I have come to pour out My spirit upon this torn flesh of yours and resurrect holiness in your life. My people have been wounded and cannot clearly see My ways. They have not known My thoughts and they have not acknowledged the special calling I have for those who have consecrated themselves for My purpose, and have *suffered for it.*

"Your father *did* love you; he just didn't know how to show it. Your mother is a good woman; she just didn't know how to let go. Your friends were only wandering spectators who wanted to know why you loved Me so much. So be healed, tonight. Your half-brother teased you because you were easy to tease, and because he couldn't accept who *he* was. Your home felt empty of love because it was void of prayer. You were molested because of the abundance of sin. You were rejected by your peers so that you could be left alone with Me and receive your long-awaited deliverance. You were alienated from your dreams because you couldn't look beyond the problem long enough to excel or achieve. You were ignored by your brothers in Christ because, (you know the reason)—they're hurting, too. You were whispered about by your aunt because, long before you were old enough to remember, she was hurt herself. I have given you good fortune, and a good, honest, respectable ancestry. Your father was a man of God. He obeyed My laws and hearkened unto My voice. He named you "Jacob" or "Deceiver," but I have *all* power and rulership over those who are Mine, and those who shall be Mine. And when I make up My jewels, Jacob, you *shall* be Mine. And from this moment,

> *...Thy name shall be called no more Jacob, but Israel: for as a prince hast thou power with God and with men, and hast prevailed* (Genesis 32:28).

Today, God is raising up princes who have lived their lives outside of the proper and destined character of their royal name. As you ask the question, "Who am I?" remember this: Psychological premises, educated guesses, sociological deductions, and biological diagrams have no principle, no posture, and certainly no power that exceeds God's omnipotence.

The very first thought of Chapter One admonished you to search this thought: if you want to know who man is, then ask his Creator. The revelation is certain not to return void when, after you have endured the wrestling with the Father, He renames you for your own continuity of life, your understanding of yourself, and your special place in the Kingdom. When He speaks, today, He speaks into your heart the royalty of your new, true name. He who endures this night of wrestling will be separated from the bruises obtained from fighting through life, that have held us back, and that have caused us to take far too long in reaching our goals.

This final hour is to confirm that your new anointed name of victory signifies the final end of "boyhood" and confirms that you are indeed mighty in Him, Who by His mercifully kind endowment of love makes us *men*.

Breaking of Day

Chapter Nine

Settle the Issue

After a night like tonight, it is no time to let go of God. You can let go and live without your fears, but after last night, you cannot possibly let go and live without God.

When God ultimately looks at the injustice done to you, as He did with Jacob, He speaks a warning word of deliverance: "Something is going to happen tonight that you are not going to understand." You're going to have to mention names. You're going to have to go back to the very places that you have deliberately avoided. "Until the breaking of day" submits a "grace period" for us to either reach into our past and tell the Lord all, or for Him to take us back and for *Him* to tell us all! He knoweth all because He searches our hearts even when we are not conscious of the effects of our own pain (see Rom. 8:27). From whichever direction your fears assail you, the Hand that will confront is the same Hand that will command the blessing of your life upon you. Being up front with your own fears only makes tonight twice as dreadful, and the greatest brother-to-brother counsel I can offer at such a time is to simply give up trying to find your own way through the dark. When you come face-to-face with your fears, let the Creator guide you! One way or another, in the morning it will be over and your chance of a lifetime will have passed you by, unless you prepare to discuss the realities that have brought you night after night of confusion, ridicule, insecurity, anger, and strife.

In just a few moments, the wrestling will cease.

You see, God had to leave because it was the breaking of day. Had He remained, Jacob would not have been able to stand before Him and view His face.

And he said, Thou canst not see My face: for there shall no man see Me, and live (Exodus 33:20).

To consider the fact that the wrestling culminated at this moment, with fifty minutes left until the breaking of day, is to consider that you, my wounded brother (and sister), have been baptized into the timing of God. That's why *tonight is the night.* Certainly during the night, God, Who wrestled to get a direct answer from Jacob, could have destroyed him, but He was merciful to him and removed his pain without wiping him out. Pride, arrogance, and stubbornness that borders on willful disobedience would have put Jacob under the severe wrath of God; he would have been completely destroyed long before the culmination of the night. His lips uttered, "I don't want this night to happen," but the meditations of his hurting soul contradicted the resistance. With a greater passion he admitted, "I need you, God."

In the next forty minutes, I beg you to let go. You've got to "let go" in order to "let God." When a man "lets God," he'll *please God.* This will mark the initial sign of being "grown up" in Him. Yes, this also means to willfully and lovingly submit to the irritability of being told what to do by another man. To settle the issue means to rest in the arms of God, even when you cannot "steal away to Dad." The issue will begin to finally settle when you heed to the calling that will lead you onto the path that points back to holiness. You will know the issue is being resolved when you decide to admit to God the situation that molded and made you this way in the first place. Then healing will begin.

If you are convinced that "God has not given us the spirit of fear; but of power, and of love, and of a sound mind"

(2 Tim. 1:7), you will make provision for all of your distress to be drenched in the love of God, removed and forgotten—forever. But it must also be confessed with the mouth.

You must be able to *say it* in the presence of the Lord. Make the choice today of who you will be: Will you continue to mope through life, and be shaken by the opinion of who men say you are? Or will you take hold of the hand of the Father, who will rumble the secrets out of you, and by the openness of His trust and promise, mend you back together into a whole *man*? He wants to bless you, give you a new name, and help you live up to who He says you are. The choice is yours, and there is only 35 minutes left to do so.

Tribulations come to equip us with strength, and make us durable soldiers for Christ. Tests come to make us stronger, and to put our words where our worship is—or where it belongs—hand in hand. We wrestle, however, with One Who is greater than you and I. Man's stubbornness calls for the remedy of wrestling. Man has not learned to cordially respond to the God of his salvation, who extends the goodwill, favor, and open invitation for man to cast all his cares upon Him; for He cares for him (see 1 Pet. 5:7). Surely, God still blesses in the middle of catastrophe. If you throw up both hands, God will help you. However, you cannot have a hidden agenda. You cannot hide things. You must come to God *honest*.

The entire dialogue of the night, although full of fury and confrontation clearly says through the voice of the Lord, "I care." Seek the Lord for your new name tonight, my brothers. Though you must first pay the price of giving in to His cross-examination, the verdict will be in your favor, if you only vow to tell the truth, the whole truth, and nothing but the truth—yes—*so help you God!* And He will.

Just think: God loves you enough to reach all the way back into your childhood and pull up things that you wish you could forget but have affected your entire life to the point whereby it's not that easy to put it behind you. When God visits you in the night, He will do whatever it takes to finalize your complete deliverance.

Thirty more minutes, my brother. Just a few more burning truths that need to be uncovered tonight, my sister.

Does this solemn hour ring out a repeated testimony that continues to stand up and claim you have been delivered when in fact, you have not? Have you avoided the *real issues* by superficially casting them under the blood of Jesus but not verbally confessing them to the Power thereof that will permanently remove them? Remember, to understand the chains of this dilemma which you are trying to shake off is to first understand the background of pain from whence you've come.

It is important to realize that Isaac developed his behavior patterns through having been influenced by the unresolved conflicts with his half-brother and the ungodly relationship of his father. Again I ask: Who can question the valiant display of courage upon Mount Moriah between Abraham and Isaac? And yet, who can doubt that Jacob, son of Isaac, is now overwhelmed with real pain? Jacob, although by this time the father of many sons, was still responsible for his actions, his inhibited feelings, and his acting out of these feelings. All of the issues of disappointment in Jacob's life were not only completely removed, but God continued to appear unto Jacob to reinforce his new identity (Gen. 35:10).

Seven years after Jacob had walked into the newness and purity of his God-given identity, he was blessed to receive the birth of his last son. Three full years had passed after wrestling with the angel, just long enough for him to have become comfortable enough with himself. Little did he know that Rachel would not survive her labor of bringing forth their newborn son. How equally tragic that Rachel would die after calling her son by the wrong name. She called him "Benoni" meaning "son of my sorrow." But the new Jacob, the restored, renamed, reminded, and re-inforced, Jacob (Israel) took the babe and called him "Benjamin" which is to say, "Son of my right hand." Once upon a time Jacob would not have been able to wisely handle such a trauma. But he told God what was wrong. "Benjamin" would become the strength of his father. How so? You know why—because his father, who had spent five-and-a-half hours talking to the Lord, had *said so*. In a matter of moments, Benjamin was removed from the danger of having to live a life with a name that indirectly charged him with his mother's death, to a life under a name that let him know clearly who he was destined to become. He was a boy who would become a proud blessing to his father and a rich seed in Israel.

Jacob's change into a prince elevated his family to their rightful place of royalty in the sight of God. As a deceiver he was incapable of carrying out the promise. As a halting prince, he found himself leaning on faith again, the Abraham principle still intact; "I wilt not let Thee go."

When God comes to meet you (and He will) upon your bed of emotional affliction, when He reaches down with His mighty hands to wrestle out of you the truth, the past, and the pain, *you must let go*. There are special things, places, and miracles that the Father wants to give you; however, He *cannot* because in the back of your mind, you're still "Jacob." You're still going to act like him. The issue needs to be conclusively settled and when it is, the healing will continue. But there are only twenty minutes left.

Haven't your dilemmas stretched you back and forth long enough? Hasn't your soul, weary of torment, insisted, "If you have to wrestle me down all night Lord, get it out of me." He may take you all the way back to those first sexual experiences that were not proper, nor godly. He'll take you back to the time you were afraid to tell your mother that your uncle had touched you in the wrong place.

He will take you back to the time when your brother fooled with and fondled you when he was supposed to be changing your underclothes. He'll take you back to those confusing moments when you struggled so hard in life to get a grip on your masculinity by trying to prove, through hurting and using women, that you were a man. Shake off the guilt and personal blame for everything that you will come face to face with and believe, for your own peace and contentment, that the wrestling *isn't about you.* As the Lord grapples with your pains, seek for a deeper understanding of the motive. The wrestling is about your baptism into the timing of God Who is eager to raise you up into the spheres of royalty, tonight! And the healing continues.

In 15 minutes the sun will be up, and either your life will change by being submitted to the Lord or it will remain tarnished by inner conflicts. Can't you feel the presence of the Lord knocking upon the altar of your heart, " 'Will you but let Me touch the hollow of your thigh' (see Gen. 32:25) and fasten you down to the conquest of My mercy by taking you away from your own strength and moving it out of joint?"

When He does, you will walk with "the limp" that we discussed at the opening of this testimony in Chapter One. But don't be embarrassed by your limp. Those who mock it do not know or understand where you have been, nor can they appreciate and share the deliverance it has brought you. Without delay, your name will consecrate you with an incentive to live up to for the rest of your life. When you see another brother limping, you will know that he too has been wrestled with, newly named, and completely delivered! The challenge for you is to bond with him, enter into brotherly covenant, and *propagate the message of God's mercies toward suffering mankind—to others who hurt.* "When thou art converted, strengthen thy brethren" (Lk. 22:32b). Explain to them that the soreness of a limp is far more desirable than the painlessness of spiritual paralysis. Like a hero, tell them what happened to you, otherwise your new name carries no meaning.

Remember, you're not the only one who has carried years of pain. Tell them Who dug it all out of you and how much better you felt when you admitted everything. Let them see the praise upon your face, and your new enthusiastic spirit toward *true worship* that your royal release has brought. And the healing will spread.

Tomorrow has no agenda of promises, and in the context of your change, it means nothing. *Tonight* settle the issue, my brother. Sell out to the Lord. Maintain your creed that you should not and will not become another statistic. Will you determine in your heart that when the arm of the Lord has moved mightily, and when the mouth of the Lord has spoken the conclusive end of your crises, *it is over?*

He has come to end your crises, to father you, to defend you. His healing abides. To "settle it" means to punctuate it with an irreversible "Yes" to the direction, confrontation, and strategy of the Lord—along with the promise to "never look back". That's the arrangement. He who is secure enough in himself at this last hour to submit to the Father that he *will not look back,* is agreeing to his own portion of true holiness and better ministry. And the healing abides.

God is preparing you to meet with Him, alone, in the face of His mercy. "Who am I?" you are still asking. Tonight will you look to the Lord and learn your new name? Perhaps *you* have been living under a false name. Throughout your life, you have been walking under an anointing of failure; you have helplessly worn a mask over your face that

God didn't put there. When you settle the issue that you will let God in, He will pull the mask off. Allow Him to deal with you, *just the way you are*, the real you. His presence is not violent; it is merciful and loving. When the day breaks (that time is almost here) you will be able to say, "It is of the Lord's mercies that we are not consumed."

Yes, for the first time in your life, things will be peacefully settled. You will be able to declare that in Him you live, you move, and have your being (see Acts 17:28). Settle the issue by telling Him the nature of the disappointment and the root of the pain. As He wrestles the pain out of you, for the first time in your life you will be able to say, "Perhaps my mother didn't make me feel wanted, and my father made me feel like his enemy, but God has come to make me feel like the son of God!" (see 1 Jn. 3:2) I will be the Father you never had. "Thou shalt call Me, My father..." (Jer. 3:19b).

Finally, settle the issue by admitting to Him the situation that hurt you the most. When you do, He will hold you in His arms and listen to what you have to say *all night long.* The day will break, soon, and for the first time you will truly understand that "the thief cometh not, but for to steal, and to kill, and to destroy," but the Lord has come that you "might have life, and...more abundantly" (see Jn. 10:10). Settle the issue, by not resisting His compassionate, loving authority; for the first time you will be able to smile, laugh, and freely and *honestly* say, "Those things don't bother me anymore. I am not the same person, for I do not identify myself by the same name."

There are only ten minutes left before daybreak. Will you refuse to let go and live life falsely, or will you let go and live as a prince, as a member of a royal nation of people who do know their God, and who *are strong* and who *shall* do mighty exploits? The saddest stories ever told are of those who, after the fact weep, "I wish I would have."

The things you have admitted to God on tonight have been a long time coming.

Therefore, my brethren dearly beloved and longed for, my joy and crown, so stand fast in the Lord, my dearly beloved (Philippians 4:1).

I pray, my brothers (and sisters who have lovingly peeked into the private chambers of the spiritually withdrawn) that you have been positively persuaded that *one of the greatest tragedies of life is to run head first into yourself.* May the Lord be merciful unto each of us and spare us from such a life-shattering collision.

What's Wrong, Jacob?

What Else Is Wrong?

Bibliography

Barnhart, C.L. *The American College Dictionary.* New York, NY: Random House, 1964.

Buhler, Rich. *Pain and Pretending: Discovering the Causes of Your Codependency.* Nashville, TN: Thomas Nelson Publishers, 1991.

Collins, Gary R. *The Rebuilding of Psychology: An Integration of Psychology and Christianity.* Wheaton, IL: Tyndale Publishers, Inc., 1977.

Di Sante, Carmine. *Jewish Prayer, The Origins of Christian Liturgy.* New York, Mahwah, N.J.: Paulist Press, 1985, pp. 19,91.

Dobson, Ted. *"Healing the Tear in the Masculine Soul"* SRVC Vision, April, 1985.

Dolby, Gordon. *Father and Son: The Wound, The Healing, The Call to Manhood.* Nashville, TN: Thomas Nelson Publishers, 1992.

Dolby, Gordon. *Healing the Masculine Soul: An Affirming Message for Men and the Women Who Love Them.* Dallas, Texas: Word Publishing, 1988.

Edersheim, Alfred. *The Life and Times of Jesus the Messiah.* Grand Rapids, MI: Wm. B. Eerdmans Publishing Co., 1971.

Excell, Joseph S. *The Biblical Illustrator* (Volume 1). Grand Rapids, MI: Baker Book House.

Heller, David. *The Soul of a Man.* New York, NY: Ballantine Books, 1990.

Hicks, Robert. *The Masculine Journey: Understanding the Six Stages of Manhood.* Colorado Springs, CO: NavPress Publishing Group, 1993.

Hicks, Robert. *Uneasy Manhood: The Quest for Self-Understanding.* Nashville, TN: Oliver Nelson Books (A Division of Thomas Nelson Publications), 1991.

Josephus, Flavius. *Complete Works of Josephus* translated by Wm. Whiston. Grand Rapids, MI: Kregel Publications, 1991.

Keil, C. F. and Delitszch, F. *Commentary on the Old Testament.* Grand Rapids, MI: Hendrickson Publishers, Inc./William B. Eerdmans Publishing Company, 1996.

Levinson, Daniel J. *The Seasons of a Man's Life.* New York, NY: Ballantine Books, 1978.

MacLaren, Alexander. *Expositions of Holy Scripture.* Grand Rapids, MI: Baker Book House.

Henslin, Earl R. *Man to Man: Helping Fathers Relate to Sons and Sons Relate to Fathers.* Nashville, TN: Thomas Nelson Publishers, 1992.

Mendez, David. *Psychology and Biblical Counseling.* Jacksonville, FL: Logos International Publishing Company, 1989.

Nee, Watchman. *The Release of the Spirit.* Cloverdale, IN: Sure Foundation Publishers, 1965.

Mish, Frederick C. (Editor-in-Chief). *Webster's Ninth Colegiate Dictionary.* Springfield, MA: Merriam-Webster, Incorporated, 1988.

Olsen, Paul. *Sons and Mothers.* New York, NY: Ballantine Books, 1981.

Payne, Leanne. *Crisis in Masculinity*. Wheaton, IL: Crossway Books, 1985.

Restak, Richard. *The Brain: The Last Frontier.* New York, NY: Warner Communications, Inc., 1979.

Salomon, Rabbi Yaakov, and Weinrib, Rabbi Yonah. *Bar Mitzvah: Its Observance and Significance*. Brooklyn, NY: Mesorah Publications, Ltd., 1991.

Shankle, Randy. *The Merismos*. Marshall, TX: Christian Publishing Services, Inc., 1987.

Strong, James *The Comprehensive Concordance of the Bible*. Lake Wylie, SC: A Christian Heritage Publishing Company, Inc., 1988.

Thompson, Keith. "The Meaning of Being Male—A Conversation wtih Robery Bly." *L.A. Weekly*, (August 5-11, 1983) p. 17.

Weust, Kenneth S. *Wuest's Word Studies*. Grand Rapids, MI: Wm. B. Eerdmans Publishing Company, 1973.